DATE DUE

APR 2 6 2018	
JUL 3 1 2018	
~~WITHDRAWN~~	

BRODART, CO.

Cat. No. 23-221

Forty-Nine Days

A Sensuous Journey in the
Modern Afterlife

Christel Janssen

SPONTANEOUS MOVEMENT PRESS

ISBN:

ISBN: 0692871144
ISBN-13: 978-0692871140

Library of Congress Control Number: 2016920075

SPONTANEOUS MOVEMENT PRESS

Contents

Part 2

Part 3

For Mama,

and all the ones that lost their loved one

Acknowledgements

THIS BOOK COULD not have been created without the many ways this story was supported in the ten years it took me to write it. So much gratitude to everyone that was part of this journey; you know who you are, in this world and the other.

A special thanks to:

Esther de Koning for being there at the early writing in Dutch.

Adikanda for touching the depth of the whole experience in your transmission. Ashley Ramsden, from the School of Storytelling for awakening the need in me to write it in English.

Leonard Orr, for believing in eternal life, and asking me over and over again if it was ready.

Ann Randolph for letting it come out of me like a beast.

Laura Lentz for your passion and your incredible magical Thursday night writing group in your Kilauea living room. Genoa Bliven, Limor Farber and all those talented writers. My Dutch friends for always believing in me, especially Simone Bleeker, Tejo Verstappen, Monique Mulder, Eliane van Dijk, Liesbet Geylvoet, Constance Cox, and Greet Dol.

All my retreat guests in Hawaii, all my students in the Virtual School for Spontaneous Movement, thank you for daring to listen.

Thank you all who believed me, and also all the ones who didn't: it appeared it didn't change my experience.

Thank you, Shen Hongxun, for being such an inspiration, and thank you for your always-expansive ways.

Thank you, Tania Casselle at KN Literary Arts for your editing. Thank you Judy Tsuei, John Teschner, my niece Ellen Janssen, Paul Brewer, Jolene Van der Steen, Constance Cox, Mike and Patty Schwartz, Diane Leone, Tom Conlee, Lana Olson and Aki Friedman for your invaluable recommendations and edits. Thank you Kauai Writers Conference for the agents that believed in me.

Thank you, Hawaii: Big Island for your wildness, Waikiki for the unknown water and Kauai for your birthing ground.

Clea Betlem, for your photography and seeing me.

Philip Glass for your music, always in the background, I cannot write without it.

And thank you, my little family, for all your love and giving me the space to write: My partner Shook, daughter Sky, and dog Layka, now Roxy.

Author's Note

NOTHING IN THIS book is made uglier or more beautiful than how I experienced it. It is a raw and honest recollection of my experiences and it is too absurd to make up.

I have tried to recreate events, locales, and conversations from my memories of them and many saved chat conversations. To maintain their anonymity, I have changed the names of individuals and places. I may have changed some identifying characteristics and details—such as physical properties, occupations, and places of residence—but the essence of the story is unedited.

One morning you wake up and say:
"It was just a fairy tale."
You laugh at yourself, but deep down you're not laughing at all.
You know that fairy tales are the only truth of life.
—Antoine de Saint-Exupéry

"…And so when the moment came
for his choosing
when his spirit refused to depart the body
refused to leave behind
what he felt was undone
it was you
he sought
it was you
who appeared at the window
for no one else in his life
had the ability to hear
what he had to say
and there was no one else he wished
to be at his side

You who have often walked between worlds
were ready for him
ready to accept his need
ready to believe in what he himself
did not comprehend
ready to greet with love
what would bring others
only fear
and together you forged a connection
that was beyond form
and yet chose to be expressed in form
in the spirit
of the trickster
once again giving voice
to that which denies
all we are accustomed
to believe…"

Transmission by ©Adikanda

Prologue

"I CAN SEE you! Can you see me?" a mischievous voice calls out loud.

I hold my breath, excited and anxious at the same time. I am sitting up in my bed, waiting for my mother to tuck me in. I stare with wide-open eyes through the dusky room. I scour the dark corner behind my bed, the cabinet with a moon-shaped shadow on it, and the painting on the wall that always seems to come alive.

"Some flowers only smell at night," my mother said earlier that day. On this warm summer night, the windows are wide open, and the scent of honeysuckle enters my room.

"No, look over here," I hear the voice sing again in a high pitch. I can clearly tell it's coming from outside.

The blue-green cedar tree stands heavy against the night sky, directly in front of my window. Darkness looms in its branches. I sit up straighter than before. Kicking the sheets off my feet, I can feel the warmth of the sun radiating out of my skin. The blackbird in the tree starts to sing its evening song. His melody swoops up and down, up, down, down, down.

"Here!" I hear the voice again. This time, its tone is impatient. I see a figure appearing between the thick branches. Like mist or a cloud of smoke, a face emerges about halfway up the tree, right above the birdhouse. It is a man, somehow familiar. My body feels softer as I stare curiously at the vague presence.

Then I see him coming out of the dark blue sky, straight through the cedar, through the clouds. I see him coming into my room, right through the middle of the open window. There's a soft buzzing sound from the almost invisible wings, like a fairy, as he comes directly toward me. I stretch out my little finger, and he quickly folds his wings as he lands on my finger, so that there's only a little bug left. The little green bug, crawling up to the top of my finger, has fragile little feet, tentacles sticking forward, and a triangular shield on his back. Its smell is so overwhelming that I don't know if I like it or not, but I am intrigued.

"Mom, come!" I yell, and I hear the fast clicking of her heels on the hard white tiles. The smell has me tumbling back into unfamiliar memories, reminding me of something I cannot grasp. It's so present, so big.

My belly tingles with excitement. My breath breaks into a fast pace. A sense of soda bubbles in my veins. Everything bubbles on the inside. It hits me in a moment. This presence, this figure, this face presenting itself now in this little animal is showing what makes it familiar. Even though we've never met, I recognize that he is my uncle. My mother's brother who never got to live. Who she never even met. And I know him, with all that I am. I tumble deeper and deeper into old memories, like horses running around us in wide fields.

"Mom!" I keep yelling. "Look, Mom!"

She comes hurrying in and kneels next to my bed.

I stare for a moment at her red-painted lips. "Look, Mommy, look!" I point at my left finger. I am sure she can see it too. I am sure she will get it and see all this little creature is.

I put my finger in front of her face, right in front of her eyes. I turn the bug slowly around and open my mouth, marveling at what I'm holding. Her blue eyes gaze at the top of my little finger. Her long eyelashes blink quickly. I tell myself she will recognize him—just like I do. She will hear the whispering like I do and recognize it as almost family.

"Oh, what a stench!" my mother says in disgust. "It's a stinkbug." She grabs it in one move and puts her thumb and index finger around it. She crushes it with her red nails, throwing what is left through the open window.

My mouth drops open. I freeze, a cry silenced in my lungs. I feel myself screaming a deep and silent "noooooo!"

"Come, let me tuck you in."

"But, Mommy, that bug is—"

"Just a bug," she declares.

I feel a shield cover my eyes, like the hard shield that was just crushed in front of me. The blanket feels too tight around my body. Things become blurry. I feel I am sinking to the bottom of the ocean, like a treasure that is ready to be lost forever. Covered by sand. Scattered in pieces. The shield of denial, like wings now covering my eyes. Shadows enter the room, and I can still sense the smell lingering. That smell of green connects me to the cloud in the tree.

The water is running in the bathroom as my mother washes her hands. She flushes the experience away; the only green she can see is in the bar of soap in her hands. Her thoughts are somewhere else: downstairs with the dishes that need to be done, with my tired father, with our broken car.

Part 1

The Shower

I LOVE THIS outdoor shower! Here under the traveler's palm, next to ginger flowers and red hibiscus on the gray pebble stones in the dark night, I turn the heat up a little again. Ah, my skin has turned to chicken skin. More chicken skin. This is how I love it the most: hot, hot water pouring down. In the middle of the rain. Holding my arms tightly folded against my body, swaying my hips. Eyes closed as I muse about the day and my guests.

This time they are two psychologists. Tall, dark Sandra and short, blonde Jennie, freshly arrived last night from my homeland Holland, have come to stay with me on a retreat. For ten days, I will do Qigong with them each morning, dive down to meet the dolphins, feel the heat of the lava flow of the Kilauea crater, and breathe with the stars on top of the snow-covered Mauna Kea. And something magical happens during those days; it always does, for them and for me.

Oh, how I love the Big Island. I relax in the shower. It is so good to be back! Back in my new life. Finally back from busy Honolulu, from the hassle of becoming a permanent resident. Finally back on my Hawaiian island.

The strong smell of the night-blooming jasmine penetrates my nostrils. I open my eyes for a moment to locate the plant and inhale the smell. It is too dark to see where the scent is coming from. I close my eyes again and for a moment my thoughts drift back to Waikiki and to my ex-lover Umberto. The lover I finally said good-bye to a week ago. That is over now too. I sigh.

I cannot help but feel Umberto's hands on my body. First faint, but then unmistakably strong. I smile, his strong, dark fingers now cupping my hips. Him behind me. Softly swaying me in the shower. I feel aroused. It feels so real. I open my eyes, almost believing I will see his fingers on my hips. But I can only see the water drops sliding down my skin in the silvery reflection of the moonlight. Hmmm, strange. Is it just imagination? I close my eyes again, throwing my head back toward the shower, the water now pouring down on my face. Yet I can still feel the so-familiar hands, moving gently up and down my curves, then stopping to give me a gentle squeeze, the way I know so well.

I shake my head in disbelief and turn it to the side. The next moment, I feel a bite on my neck; it is his bite. It is like he is swirling his body around me. Wow. My memory of him is so alive. My skin feels so alive, as if touching his dark skin. Like he touched me so many times back in Waikiki. The hot water from the shower is still pouring down. With my eyes closed, I can now see all of him. The shade of his dark skin, the way his strong arm muscles are filled out, his Hawaiian face, and above all, his eyes, his endless eyes.

He is so real now, so intertwined with me. I feel his touch, his pressure against my lower body, so realistic that my womb contracts in reaction. The next moment he … penetrates. Reflexively, I turn up the heat of the shower a little more.

More chicken skin … the rain pouring down harder now. That is so weird. It feels so real. I can feel him inside of me—his strong penis—even though he is hundreds of miles away. Umberto is on Oahu, another island. I open my eyes again and then close them quickly as I feel myself carried away by the sensations. Moving, moving in and out of me. I am dripping from the inside. Feeling so hot. My breath starts to deepen. Tingling sensations run up and down my burning vagina.

Sandra and Jennie are on the lanai just on the other side of the house, waiting for dinner. Umberto is moving faster and faster in and out of me now, my hips moving with him. My lower body gushes with this delicious, tense warmth. I am overflowing with pleasure as the rain stops. Sex … the only thing that was really good between us, so magical. I open my eyes, blinking a few times, and then I turn off the pretty copper knob and get out of the shower.

***

2

"I just have to check my e-mail!" I yell as I walk up the blue stairs to my bedroom after dinner, my sarong still wrapped around my body. My room feels comfortable and warm as I overlook Kealakekua Bay: "the pathway of the gods" in Hawaiian. I take a deep breath. A little sliver of moon reflects on the dark water. This is my favorite view from the house. The house I have already been caretaking for friends for nine months now, until they can sell it.

I hope we get to swim with the dolphins in front of the house tomorrow morning.

I open my laptop. The laptop starts up on my bed while I go through my clothes to get dressed. I admire my naked body in front of the mirror for a moment, imagining again Umberto's dark velvet body next to mine. It is as if I can still feel the excitement I felt earlier before dinner. It was so real.

Pling. The computer sounds behind me to let me know there is a message. Strange … the only person I message with is Umberto, and we stopped talking when I left Oahu. I jump onto my bed to read it.

"Hello, Christel. This is Aran."

I am vaguely surprised, confused. Aran is Umberto's brother, but I've never talked to him before. *Why now?*

"We tried to reach you, but your phone was off all day, so we do it this way. Sorry to tell you, but Umberto had a heart attack earlier today. He was in a coma for a few hours and passed away at seven thirty. Sorry to have to tell you this way. We will keep you informed about what is going to happen."

In a trance, I look at the phone on my bed—still turned off so as to not be disturbed during the retreat. I stare at the clock on my computer; it is exactly nine o'clock. Seven thirty. That was just one and a half hours ago. Things start to get blurry as I try to grasp the words. *Heart attack? Coma? Passed away? Umberto?* He was never sick or weak. He never showed any signs of pain. *Why?* Inside me, I feel a breaking. Tears start squeezing out of my eyes; there's no stopping them. This man with whom I've had such a strange relationship has died. It cannot be true! My disbelief is fighting my tears.

My breathing stops, and I stare blankly at the curtains with the green and orange Hawaiian motif, gently moving up and down by the wind.

The palm trees in the background have lost their noise. A cold draft wraps around my shoulders. I had just calculated the other day how long our relationship had lasted, and I came up with forty-nine.

Forty-nine days that we actually spent together in Waikiki. The next moment, I am reminded that forty-nine days is how long a soul spends in Bardo, as Jhampa, the Tibetan man had told me long ago when I began my career in traditional Chinese medicine. Bardo is the in-between state between earth and sky. Forty-nine days of the soul wandering in an in-between state after death. And now, Umberto is right there!

I get up in a haze, feeling the urge to go downstairs. I grab my laptop and clamp it firmly against me, determined not to let go of the source of the message. Will there be another message from Aran? I don't even have his phone number. My heart is beating in my throat while my hand grasps the blue railing. Halfway down, I see for a moment my two guests on the lanai, unsuspectingly sipping their glasses of wine. The dinner plates are still on the table. *Shall I tell them?* I take a deep breath.

Sandra is the first one to see me. "Hey? Are you okay?"

I go down the last steps and silently flop on the chair, my back toward the dark garden. I swallow, a big lump in my throat.

Desperately I look at Sandra, searching for words. Jennie's red, burnt face starts to turn pale around her pointy little nose. The white lines around her eyes are showing even more as her fingers grab for her box of cigarettes; she never takes her gaze off of me.

I cannot hold it together anymore. I burst into tears again and bow my head while sliding my laptop onto the table. The grief seems to gush out of me even more. Sandra and Jennie look at me with big eyes.

"What happened?" Sandra asks again.

"Message," I whisper with a finger pointing at my laptop as the cause of my reaction. Then I collect myself, clear my throat and say, "Umberto, my boyfriend in Honolulu … had a heart attack today … fell into a coma … and now, he has died …" I burst into tears again in a vain attempt to make a coherent story.

"I did not know you had a lover," Jennie says as she pulls a cigarette out of the box.

Sandra looks briefly at her as though to say, "What is that remark about?"

"Yeah, er, well ... *lover* is not the right word. It's more a past lover ... a lover I had when I was still in Waikiki." My attention is pulled to my monitor, a second ago showing a homemade picture of Kealakekua Bay, here right in front of us; the little specks in the middle are two dolphins. In a flash, the image of the ocean begins to vibrate and then the whole picture and so too does the Yahoo Messenger screen that is still open in the picture below with Aran's message. Everything on the screen goes black, like the test screen that appears on televisions, and only noise remains. Everything appears far away and in slow motion.

I hold my breath as I look at what is taking place on the monitor screen. My eyes open wide, not wanting to miss anything. The screen flickers while still dark; suddenly, from that darkness, something emerges. Large handwritten letters in white on the screen, as if ink is dripping from it.

"Why are you crying?" It is handwritten in cursive. Outside any computer framework or window. Across the screen of my two-year-old heavy HP computer from Costco. One inch high. The small box in which I had typed to Aran is still showing the messages on the bottom right corner of my screen.

Is something wrong with my computer? My logical mind searches in panic for an explanation. I swallow. My mouth feels dry, and my body stiffens on the chair. Then, my breath breaks and I am flooded with emotions, like a tidal wave. My attention is drawn to the ocean, and for a moment, I hear a wave violently crashing on the rocks. Strange ... the ocean was otherwise so quiet today.

This is Umberto! Like a loud bell inside, it hits me. I don't know why, but I know it for a fact.

Disbelief and resistance fade to the background, and a huge calmness emerges in me.

"Just answer," I hear a whisper from within say.

I type in the text box where the conversation with Aran is still open, unsure of how else I can communicate back.

"Who is this?"

"Hello, Christina Ingrid Janssen," again appears in large letters. My birth names! My birth names have just come in that crazy big handwriting on the screen!

I feel him again. Our connection so deeply ingrained somehow—this

5

Hawaiian Papuan man. The sense of belonging together takes over, despite our separation. I see his dark skin between the white sheets. The black, thick, long curly hair moving through the crystal blue water, the pinkness of his feet as he dives down, his exoticness. And now, our connection echoes through these strange letters vibrating on my screen. I take a deep breath.

It continues.

"I am Umberto. I am here in heaven. I'm dancing with angels. But why are you crying?"

In heaven? How can you communicate with me? You can actually see that I am crying? My mind is running in all directions. I look directly into the questioning eyes of Sandra and Jennie and suddenly become aware of their presence. The pristine feeling of our day is shattered, and I know I am not able to hold it together right now—even though we still have nine more days in our retreat.

"What's going on?" they seem to say with their cold faces.

I swallow. Without uttering a word, I turn the screen toward them. I see their eyes widen and their faces turn white. Sandra's mouth opens, but nothing seems to come out. Jennie takes a step back from the screen with horror on her face.

Day 1: The Meeting

THE METAL GATE closes with a loud bang as I step outside the King Kamehameha apartment building. This is the twelve-story building in Waikiki where I am living with my friend and lover Lennard for a few weeks until I move back to the Big Island. The bang resonates in the little hallway behind me. It awakens the nerves along my spine. A strange mix of anxiety and anticipation runs up and down my back, and my legs are shaky. *Did I bring my phone? Key?* I sigh, relieved, as my fingers reach the cool metal of my phone in my purse.

"Call me when you need me. I will come and get you," Lennard said.

We have an open relationship, and with the freezer door half open and his long index finger in his newly created pecan, coconut, and chocolate dessert, Lennard started talking about it this afternoon: dating online. Licking his finger over and over again. "You should try it too." I don't know if it was the way I saw the milky, gooey stuff enter his mouth or if it was the way I felt the cold air from the freezer falling down on the curves of my naked middle. I thought, *If he can do it, I can too.*

Within an hour, I get a response.

Lennard says, "And now, go see what kind of flesh it is."

I sigh and take a deep breath, inhaling the evening air. I smell a mixture of exhaust pipes, sewer, and plumeria flowers from the tree next door. Looking up at the twelfth floor of the building at our apartment, I see a little figure waving enthusiastically at me, as only gay guys can wave. He is more gay than bisexual. With his oversized Hawaiian shirt and skinny arms, Lennard is yelling something down to me, but the sound gets lost between the high buildings.

Lennard is my beacon here in Hawaii. Three years ago, he immediately drew my attention at a Qigong retreat in Belgium as the only American between all these French, British, Dutch, and Norwegian students. He was the one who had the funniest laugh, bending his whole body backward while doing the standing exercise. It was like he just stepped out of the comic book *Tintin* with his white hair with a crest, boyish body, and adventurous enthusiasm. We instantly fell in love. We moved to Hawaii that same month. He moved from Los Angeles to try his luck as a standup comedian, and I moved from Holland as an acupuncturist following a strange call for Hawaii.

It is already darker than I thought it would be. The clickety-clack of my new high heels on the uneven surface of the sidewalk makes me smile. It sounds so unfamiliar after all those months of just wearing slippers on the Big Island. I will be in Waikiki for two months. I am more proud and confident with each step. Soon, Hawaii will always be at my feet—no more questioning how I'm going to make it work or how I can stay here in Hawaii forever. No more sweating and palpitations in my throat at immigration after yet another time entering the United States from Holland. These new white shoes will walk me right into my new status in Hawaii tomorrow on my wedding day with Lennard.

"Umberto," I pronounce out loud the Dutch way, now almost at the end of Kalani Avenue. Another gush of plumeria fragrance enters my nose from the tree at the corner. Umberto's profile picture was taken from the side. The profile is as generic as it can be: stocky body, Pacific Islander, born in 1972, a year younger then me, and "looking for love."

"Uuuuuumbertoooo," I try again, the English way protruding my lips. *What a strange name.*

I arrive at the Ala Wai Canal at the edge of Waikiki a few minutes early. We will just walk toward each other. "Let's meet at the Ala Wai Canal," he said in the online chat. We haven't even spoken on the phone yet. It is not even two hours ago that I first connected with this Hawaiian-Indonesian man living only two blocks away in Waikiki.

The Ala Wai Canal separates Waikiki from the rest of Honolulu. It was a swamp until high-rise buildings were put up on the tiny strip of land. It was turned in a tourist paradise with the smell of suntan lotion and bronzed bodies in little bikinis with shiny sunglasses under exotic, waving palm trees. A white beach with sand imported from Brazil and pristine blue water on one side, a dark dirty canal on the other. I walk slowly to the left along the canal. In the distance, I can see a little bench. The streetlight next to it turns on. I decide to sit down and wait. I carefully fold my dress under my thighs, pinching my leg to make it all seem more real.

A minute passes, and I start to feel uncomfortable. I smell the slight scent of rotten fish floating in the murky water in front of me, the water contaminated with chemicals and sewage. It is so polluted that somebody immediately died when he fell in not long ago. What a strange place to have a date. My eyes pierce into the water, and I see something move under the surface. I read today that Waikiki means "unknown water" in Hawaiian.

"I have a date," I say out loud to convince myself. "I have an Internet date," I say again with a laugh. I feel a slight flutter in my stomach. I had sworn I would never do Internet dating. I have never had really a date before; men just entered my path and melted into my life. I had kept myself far away from being seduced off my path, my path to becoming an inhabitant of Hawaii and finding out what that "call for Hawaii" really is about.

I wonder how it will feel again. The warmth of a hand on my naked body, the sound of the breath of a man in my ear, all the beautiful paintings in history dripping from erotica stored inside me and coming alive again, as if I were the model. The hardness of a man that awakens my body's softness in all the deep places. When I look to the left, I can see a figure walking this way. A dark silhouette, not looking up when he passes me. Wearing a hat pulled down over his face. Body leaning forward a little. The man has passed now, almost disappearing in the dark. He ambles a bit on his slippers, stops for a moment, and then turns around. Walking back to me. *Is that him?*

"Are you Christel?" he mumbles.

I will be home early tonight, I think as I feel relief in my stomach. This person doesn't give the impression that he will screw up my marriage tomorrow. I wish for one moment my friends in Holland could see me here. I can now see his face a little more, and I cannot distinguish if it is the lighting or if his face is really dark. He has a wide nose, strong bones and cheeks, like the Hawaiians, and his solid protruding brow reaches right over his dark eyes like the overhang of a cliff. He turns his eyes away from me, looking down.

"Yes, I am Christel. Are you Umberto?" He sits down a little uncomfortably, just a little too close to the edge, as if ready to run away. A slight smell of cheap aftershave and laundry soap covering a musty smell hits my nostrils. He is a little taller then me. I look at his developed forearm and his compact hand now resting on the bench. Shoulders bend forward as if protecting his heart.

"Why did you pass me at first? Didn't you recognize me? Or were you afraid?" I chuckle nervously.

"Yes, maybe that is what it was," he answers. He speaks indistinctly, as if the answer needs to be kept inside his mouth as a secret. It intrigues me somehow.

"I couldn't believe it. It is also already so dark, isn't it?"

"What?"

"You were sitting there so beautifully in the light."

"And you came as a shadow out of the dark," I joke.

He smiles at me for a moment, showing his shiny teeth. I see his eyes for the first time. There is something different about them. Brown pupils that seem to be surrounded by eye white. Floating in endless white, not defined by an upside and an underside. A little bulging maybe. Like people who are not really grounded have as I learned once in iris diagnostics. But they pull me right in, I want to float with him. The ice is broken.

I feel myself relax and grow curious about this dark man with his big eyes—not as a potential lover. I wonder who he is—the person I randomly met on the Internet who happens to sit here next to me on this bench. Under the light, along this dark black canal. In his black shorts and black shirt. Me in my brown dress with pink spots and my wedding shoes.

"Did you say you are Papuan?" My voice involuntarily breaks. "Papuan," I repeat. The darker ones, more primitive, even with a stronger sense of magic than other Indonesians. I look down at the dark body of water in front of me, bordered by a straight line of gray cement.

"Yes, I was born in Jayapura."

"Wow, I think the Dutch used to call it Hollandia."

I try to focus on the rim of his forehead, his shiny dark skin, covered by thick black hair.

"My father still has a big cocoa plantation there," he adds.

My body bounces up. "So does he make chocolate? My dad is a candy maker too, a Willy Wonka, inventing sweets." My eyes rest on his strong forearm and see it turn into a dark chocolate brown now I can almost taste the bitter-sweetness.

"No, no, no." He shakes his head shortly. "My parents are now living here in Hawaii. My mother is Hawaiian. She is born on the Big Island."

"Wow! The Big Island is where I am living too! I love the Big Island."

"So you are not living here?" He turns his head toward me, frowning his brows. The consequence of my words clouds our date. His body bends a little more forward.

I try to swallow what I have just said in a too enthusiastic voice and remember not to mention the wedding, the immigration papers, and Lennard. I kick my white shoes back under the bench, as if they would reveal my wedding, but he seems undisturbed and continues about his grandfather living in The Hague in Holland. I tell him proudly I was born in Oisterwijk, the pearl of Brabant.

Brimming with energy, I feel myself now next to him on the little bench.

The two worlds represented in him—one where I came from the other where I am going—Holland and Hawaii or even more the Big Island. The space in between us has filled up with so much. I want to absorb it all through my skin and let it penetrate my muscles. I want to feel it: the landscapes, the chocolate farm, the people, the wildness, and the mystery.

And inside of me I can now feel it all turn. After almost two years, I finally allow myself to open that door again, opening myself to a man. I finally let myself feel all there is to feel; I am curious, hungry, and thirsty to be touched and embraced. I long to belong and demand a deep connection—not like the platonic love with Lennard.

But the more the excitement starts to vibrate in my lower belly, the more I notice how this man is hunched down and holding back. "The Big Island," he mumbles now, pointing his head down again. As if he has a glimpse of something, I see him tighten his fist around it, clamping his teeth together. The tension is visible in his cheek. He shoots one leg forward—as if it is escaping from underneath the bench—and then he tucks it right back under. For a moment, I try to lean into what he really wants. I can feel him wanting to just keep it all inside, keep something all inside. *But why? And what?*

I take a deep breath. I cannot help but see them now next to each other: my last lover Ravindu, the one I met after that soul mate workshop at the Sixth Sense Center, and Umberto, exactly the same island family, same dark skin, same big, bulging, rolling eyes, same mysteriousness. Would this man be able to to lead me so astray? For a moment, I try to ignore a gnawing anxiety shooting through my belly. We are not a good match.

Day 2: The Dam

I AM ONLY going to be in Waikiki for a short time—until I am able to return to the Big Island with Lennard where my life is waiting for me. I am determined not to get distracted. My determination is like my grandmother's chin—the chin that was sticking forward in my father's whole family, especially my grandmother. I loved her for her chin, so triumphantly sticking out into the future. My father had that same chin. For me, he could do magic. He was an inventor of candies. The most romantic job a girl's father can have; he was a Willy Wonka. I haven't inherited that chin myself, but I've inherited his determination for sure.

"Hey, hello, Christel," a mumbling voice sounds behind me.

My body freezes on the warm black stones on the dam. The buzz of city and ocean fades into the background. *Umberto? No! Here?*

The moment seems to last for minutes, as if tracking all the people in Honolulu who could potentially call my name. But there are only two: my newly wed husband and … Umberto. I met Umberto four days ago, the night before my wedding. *Umberto?* Here on this side of Waikiki, the bright side? Here on the other side of my wedding and the spontaneous honeymoon to Kauai that followed right after? Here in my new future, in my new status as a married woman?

In disbelief, I stare at the ocean, the almost too perfectly curling teal blue waves of Waikiki. It had become so clear to me: We were not a good match. I should not waste time on him. The whole idea of an Internet date was ridiculous anyway. Besides, I have to go back to the Big Island. I have a house to live in, classes at the Sixth Sense Center, and luscious retreats to offer to the Dutch. Lennard will go back and forth between the islands, focusing on his real estate. Being with somebody, anybody, here on Oahu would only be a distraction for me.

Before I can turn around, he is already kneeling next to me. My arms tighten against my body as I feel resistance arise. On the walk here, along all the too-white beaches in Waikiki, I precisely formulated an e-mail in my head. I tell him about my choice, our non-match. *How did he find me right here? Right here at the edge of Waikiki? It feels like a mistake.*

"Um-berto." I look up at his strong upper legs, his black shorts, his white shirt, and his face. I cannot help but look at his neck.

"You need a much brighter lover," Lennard had said while we were doing Qigong at a beach on our honeymoon yesterday. "One that is all about stretching up his neck." He laughed, moving his head around wildly.

Dr. Shen, the Qigong grandmaster, taught us how the key to health is to emphasize stretching your neck and opening your intervertebral space so everything gets more space and nourishment: nerves, blood vessels, organs, and all parts of your life. "Gravity is pulling us down, down, down anyway. All the way down to your grave," Shen would say sarcastically.

I can feel it now in Umberto next to me. His wide brown neck is held forward—as if he is carrying a heavy weight. His shoulders are drooped, his chin is too far forward, and his whole body is hunkered down. It is being pulled down by an invisible force, a magnet stronger even than gravity.

I cannot help but stretch my neck a little more and pull in my chin. "Yes, I am more about up, up up," I had joked back to Lennard, pretending to be a giraffe.

"Hi, how are you?" Umberto says.

My eyes slide down to his sleeve. He is wearing a blue and white long sleeve shirt that actually makes him look really good. I realize this is the first time I have seen him during daylight—or at least for these few moments that the sun is still above the horizon. His forehead has a golden glow with the tiny little speckles of shimmering sweat. *What is he doing here?*

"Do you sit here often on this dam?" He laughs heartily, moving his head back in a way that makes his neck seem much more flexible. "I thought you were on Kauai?" That was the last thing I told him before my departure, in a text message the day after we met: "I am going on a business trip with Lennard to Kauai, as his real-estate assistant." He replied that he would see me when I came back. But I already made the decision—we are not going to see each other ever again. I just needed the right moment to tell him in the e-mail I was about to send tonight.

"Actually, I just came back from Kauai this morning. It was wonderful!"

"Do you like him?"

Surprised I look at him.

"What? Oh, Lennard? My roommate? The real estate agent? He is gay." I chuckle.

"Or rather bisexual." I wonder how I could ever tell Umberto about our open relationship.

"Gay?" he says like he is swallowing a hairy caterpillar, pushing away a stone with his foot.

"Yeah, what is wrong with that?"

He turns his head in front of him, curling his back up slightly as if still sensing the hairy caterpillar and wanting to spit it out.

I peer at him with concentration. Why did he have such a strong reaction?

"It's weird," he says, his face still pointing at the water.

"Um-berto," I say. I feel like my mother, a schoolteacher. Pronouncing his name is somehow showing it to me, something old-fashioned, something pushed upon him, something cultural, something Christian maybe. *Gay is wrong? Another good reason to write that e-mail.*

For a while, we just stare in front of us.

He turns his head toward me. His whole face is visible again—like that first night but in the light. His strong big head, the eyebrows, the wide Hawaiian nose—it is a pleasure to look at it. Like an exotic landscape to explore. Like how I would study a painting in the Rijksmuseum in Amsterdam. The chiaroscuro in Rembrandt's paintings. The e-mail in my head fades to the background. I look him straight in the eye.

And … there they are again. Those brown eyes that beg me to get lost in them. Never before have I seen such mysterious eyes. I don't know what to think of them really. They are not bright, sparkling, dreamy, or striking, but there is something about them. Something is hidden and unclear, like a gem buried under many veils, and it sparks my curiosity. A chill travels down my arm, and I feel that chain reaction of sensations again. It's a strange mix of where I come from and where I am going, united in this man. All the common distant connections from our background start to awaken. Above all, I feel the connections with Hawaii, his mother's love for the Big Island, and my love for the Big Island. I had wanted a deep connection when I sent out my profile on Match.com. In his eyes, I find something deep and valuable. His eyes are deep eyes, but I don't know what to think of them. Dangerous deep, unknown deep, misleading deep maybe, or tremendously rich deep.

He installs himself a little closer to me. Close enough now to be within reach and smell.

"Look," he says and points at the red sun almost touching the water. The ocean is reflecting brilliant sunrays around the surfers. His voice is so much warmer and bubblier than that first night.

What now? My thoughts are racing. I try to reproduce that e-mail in my head. It was over, but now he is sitting next to me. I am about to fall in an abyss, so dark yet tempting, asking me to jump in. It is almost impossible to prevent. I am sitting here next to him so quietly, and he is so much more attractive than the image I created in my mind when I was on Kauai. I had concluded on my honeymoon with Lennard that it was not smart to start something else. *And what about his bad posture says it all?*

Umberto is looking at the last sliver of sun. He had had a haircut, making him look really handsome—like black movie stars whose names I always forget. His cheeks are the perfect shape. His sultry inviting lips bring me back to that first kiss. That kiss that changed everything. At the end of that first night, when I felt like Cinderella, I had to run home in my wedding shoes before the clock struck twelve. He took me in his arms and kissed me, and then we kissed and kissed and kissed. He kissed all my doubt away—all the differences, all the darkness—until I ran home. *What have I done? I don't want to have anything in the way of my marriage tomorrow. We are not a good match.* It was like he had kissed me all the way from Holland to Hawaii like the next day I was kissed from Holland to Hawaii in front of the altar at my wedding with Lennard. That clumsy kiss felt so real.

"What are you looking at?"

"I just was looking at you." I look down shyly. Inside me, I can now feel it all tilt. It tumbles upside down again. The decision I so clearly made my decision on my honeymoon in Kauai. I am not going to open myself to Umberto—, or to any man. I can almost see it shatter now.

"I am curious about you. Curious about who is inside this beautiful dark skin," I say. While I am saying it, I can feel the truth of it in his eyes, inside that velvety skin, between the smell of freshly washed clothes and armpit sweat.

He smiles, reaches out his hand, and barely touches my fingers resting on the black stone. Our three fingertips now are connected. My body ignites, gushing with warmth.

"How did you like Kauai?" he says. "I love that island myself. I go there to visit my Uncle Ryan, my mother's brother. Ryan Kahananui." He tries to carry the conversation on and ignores what I just said.

"What an interesting name." I feel blue electricity through my fingers, reaching my insides, my blood, giving a pleasant squeeze in my womb.

"Can you say it again?" I try to sound as normal as possible. "Kahananui. It is my mother's name." It sounds like an exotic song.

Kahananui. Kahananui. I repeat for myself.

"How did you like Kauai?" he asks again.

Before I can answer, I see it for a split second: a black shadow right next to his head. A black spot flits like a bat. When I try to focus on it, it seems to disappear. *Is it just my imagination? Is it related to him wanting to skip the question about Kahananui? There it is again!* Like a swarm of flies, little speckles hover in the air next to his head. I sometimes get a glimpse of energies around a person's head when I give a reading at the Sixth Sense Center, usually like little lights sparkling. "Essence points," a friend called it once.

In the almost two years that I have taken classes at the Sixth Sense Center on the Big Island, I have developed quite a skill to see these energies. I sometimes see a little cloud of dust leaving people's heads the moment something important gets hit inside of them. It looks like smoke from an overheated brain. I have never seen such a dense, cloudy appearance like the one next to Umberto's head. Everything seems glowing and shiny in the light of the sunset. "The best light to take a profile picture," Lennard would say.

Umberto's face emanates a warm, quiet glow. I am glad I don't see the cloud anymore. It has totally disappeared. I feel beautiful and strong. I stretch out my legs in front of me as if I am pushing away the last blankets of denial. I long for his touch, his taste, to kiss him again, his full lips on mine. There is no need for words. I feel myself falling into that abyss. We fall into that abyss. Umberto bends over, embracing me gently. There is this kiss again. His tongue meets my tongue; our tongues curl around each other. In that curling, all of my senses curl around him. Willingly, I lay myself down on the warm stone. I crawl into his world, and our worlds merge. I meet whole nations and groups of people. It's peculiar that I seem to know or have affinity with them.

***

On the last day of my first visit to the Big Island in May 2002, I found out about the Sixth Sense Center.

"Your spirit pulled you in here, right?" A loud deep voice spoke as a big guy with red hair almost magically appeared in front of me. Brian was the main teacher at the center. He instantly summed it up in three sentences: The whisper that told me to go to Hawaii, my feeling of being so at home, the connection with the volcano, the dolphins, my decision to move, and even my work as an acupuncturist in Holland. Earlier that day, I had decided to come back to Hawaii—and now I was sold. I had to learn to read people intuitively like he did.

Now, I cannot wait to go back to the Sixth Sense Center: Three times a week, I drive to South Point, to the little red building on the black lava rocks next to the blue ocean, to learn how to perceive energies with my eyes closed. I gather my attention in the center of my mind and open my clairaudient, clairsentient, and sixth sense abilities. In a way, it is not so different from how I learned from Dr. Shen to diagnose by mentally scanning a body during my training as a Qigong teacher and acupuncturist. Now, I learn how to interpret the energy patterns of other students, sitting opposite them with my eyes closed. I see their energy as pictures or as colors. Sometimes, there is a sudden knowingness, which Buddhist Lamas call "information transmission."

The Whisper

SOMETIMES THE WHISPER is in the waterfall, the smoke of the volcano goddess, the tree, or the sand. I like to believe it is mine and always supportive of me. The whisper—with authority, friendly, bubbly, and inviting—always invites and is never vague. Like an embrace, like the embrace in bed right before I fell asleep when I was a child. The embrace of the invisible, enveloping and uplifting. So utterly mine, elegant and tasteful. Never pushy. Dropping random notes into my life, friendly yet determined, hinting when to go forward and when to stop.

Sometimes it is under the surface of the water, disappearing and appearing—or like honey dripping into my head. Like the smell of cedar, whispering to me, loving, always loving. Sometimes in English, mostly in Dutch, sometimes in French. The whisper once told me to move to the very center of town, the center of Maastricht. It told me it was a springboard toward something new. It told me to look beyond the little house to find a place to live. That whisper told me to go to Hawaii.

***

"How did *you* end up here?" the Hawaiian with the wreath of leaves wrapped around his head looks at me fiercely. Secretly aghast, I turn around and look behind, hoping he is looking at somebody else. *"No, you!"* He points his elegant dark finger toward me.

"Erm," I stammer and look helplessly at the expectant faces next to me. I am just in time. I have been living on the Big Island for almost three months. "Lecture by Kahunas" is what I saw announced this morning. Kahunas are Hawaiian shamans. After a long two-hour drive to Waimea,

19

I am sitting in a little community center in a cool area where it rains the whole day. The Hawaiians I have met so far are all friendly. Some are a little bitter, but mostly they are indifferent, hanging around their pickup trucks and drinking beer. These Hawaiians are different.

I am still moved to tears by the woman who blew a huge shell and started dancing and singing to invoke the ancestors for the lecture. There is nothing artificial about it, although I couldn't understand a word she sang while the man was drumming the calabash. It touches me directly and deeply, plucking at my emotions.

Before I can answer him, the kahuna starts to gesture. "It was the mana, huh? The mana pulled you here!" He starts to gesture as if pulling a long rope toward him. For a moment, I imagine I am hanging on that thick rope and the mana had indeed pulled me to the island, a puppet on the strings of fate.

Like Qi for the Chinese, mana is energy for the Hawaiians. It is often associated with power or supernatural power. It is in everything: the rocks, the plants, people, and places. Through breathing exercises, your mana can increase. Hawaiians believe that some people contain more mana than others. The Ali'i, the Hawaiian royalty, are believed to be highly charged with mana. They even believe that mana can be stolen through sorcery or if someone walks in their shadow.

"Yes." I nod slowly, my body tensing with the realization. I see myself standing there again—the first time I landed in Kona and stepped on the lava, almost a year earlier. I felt the warm, sticky air, smelled the ocean, the flowers, and the welcoming warmth. That is where it happened. "Home" is what it said to me, in English, while tears ran down my cheeks, seemingly emerging out of nothing. It was as if life converged there at that point. Everything felt just right. Every cell in my body started to vibrate enthusiastically; destination reached— it sang, and not simply the destination of my twenty-four- hour journey from Holland.

The beautiful man dressed only in leaves and a loincloth continues his story.

"The call for Hawaii" he calls it. Many others share my strange urge to come to this faraway place. He starts talking about *aumakuas*, ancestors in the shape of guides. The spirit guides appear in animals, places, rocks, or people. It intrigues me and reminds me of my first encounter with a shark a year ago and the words from the Hawaiian man: "The shark is your aumakua."

Throughout the lecture, two old Hawaiian women sit in wheelchairs on the podium in front of the kahuna. With colored blankets on their knees and beautiful plumeria flowers around their necks, they look fragile and vulnerable. They seem to be asleep the whole time, and their heads hang forward almost in their laps. They haven't said a word, and the kahuna introduces these two Hawaiian women to the crowd as the two aunties. When the lecture finishes, the eldest appears wide-awake. I guess she is in her nineties.

I feel the urge to say good-bye and thank her, but I don't know for what. When I reach out my hand and it touches hers, she instantly grabs it with both hands and pulls me toward her. It fills me with surprise. I wonder if she didn't see my hand coming.

She whispers in my ear, "You think that I have been sleeping?"

I feel caught.

"No, not at all," she says. "I have been watching you." She squeezes my hands again. "You didn't come here for no reason. You have a special task. You are very, very special. You have a unique destiny that only you are suited for. Go for it! Don't get distracted! Go for it!" She speaks sternly and looks at me intently. She waves her finger in the air at me, almost scolding me for floating around too much.

I know exactly what she means, and I feel so validated. When I look more closely at her eyes, I see they have a white glow. *Maybe she is blind.* I know that it is true that she can look completely into my life, despite appearing to be both sleeping and blind—not with her regular eyes but like a helicopter from up above she saw it with her intuition. Exactly as the kahuna could see how the mana had pulled me like a rope to Hawaii. Everything he said entered me deeply. Now that I hear these words from this old aunty, I know that I somehow have way more connection with Hawaii than I ever imagined possible.

When I get up, everybody around us has left, including the other "aunty."

Only the many chairs in this little place remind me of the gathering.

What could it be that the aunty saw? Does she see me like energy? Or more like a person? Like I see people and have access to information about them. Is she also aware of two places at the same time? I experienced it so many times when I lived and worked at a floatation center in Holland, consciously noticing my energy body separate from my physical body each time I entered the tank. I wonder if she has a special technique that Hawaiian shamans use, melting your senses together into one, making them into a compressed ball as big as a marble that you can send out of your physical body to gather information far away, like my Qigong teacher had taught us.

What did she mean by go for it? It felt so true. It was as if my choice to go to Hawaii all of a sudden had been fully recognized. All the signs on my path gather together and suddenly show me a glimpse of a much bigger picture. I cannot seem to grasp this mysterious picture. What do I have to go for? What don't I have to distract myself from? She was so stern when she said, "Don't get distracted."

Dr. Shen often told me the same thing and made a gesture of cutting wires above my head. All kinds of realities were floating above my head like balloons on wires, and he was encouraging me to cut away the strings of the ones that were not relevant.

Maybe it has something to do with men. I smile. That was it when I studied with Dr. Shen. He would shake his head and say, "Don't get distracted by … *men.*"

Vegas

"I AM GOING to help you only once!" Shen had said it twice, his finger up in the air and a furious look on his face. "And I really mean it." It was after my first three months in Hawaii, and I had to go back to Holland when my tourist visa expired. I went straight to a Qigong retreat with him in Amsterdam.

"What happened to you?" Shen said, his voice a mix of disappointment and astonishment. He was looking at me sternly with his penetrating eyes. He had spotted me immediately among all the students. "Somebody stole your power. Somebody stole your *dantian*." He stared at my lower belly, and I could feel his eyes scanning me—just as he had scanned me so many times.

I wanted to say, "I stepped out of it already. I stepped out of that magician's life, that dream, Las Vegas, that house … didn't I?" I felt indeed that something was missing, something in my belly that I had gotten to know so well through all that Qigong practice. Shen would call it—the center, the core, that second brain—my dantian or my gut feeling.

Valentine's Day had never existed in my life until then. I didn't take it seriously at that Valentine's soul mate workshop at the Sixth Sense Center on the Big Island. Yet I met my soul mate on Valentine's Day in Maui at a healing center in Olinda in the mountains. Lennard had just moved to Maui, and I was visiting him. Lennard and I attended his lecture. Ravindu was long, slender, and charismatic. He had long, curly black hair and a funny accent. He was originally from an island in the Indian Ocean. He puts his mouth on people's foreheads and blows into it, giving them a life-changing experience. During a break, he stepped toward me and asked me where I was from.

Behind my back, Lennard whispered, "Ask if we can get a blow job too."

And we got it. It was the most amazing experience. He took us after everybody had left in the upstairs room. I was on a bed in the dark, and he blew into my forehead. I could feel it coming in.

"You have the purple light in you. I have to tell you something," he whispered mysteriously in my ear. "Come back tomorrow to see me."

Lennard and I drove all the way from the other side of the island to Lahaina the next day.

"You are the woman of my life, and I want you to come to with me to Las Vegas," he said after he closed the door to the living room where twenty women were waiting for their five-minute blow sessions.

Then he said, "Hee!" It was so long and drawn out. He used so many keys that it seemed like he showed me the compilation of his life and his delight at seeing me. He moved his head like a Balinese dancer. He took off his purple shirt and put his naked body next to mine. He crossed way too many boundaries in way too short a time, but I was okay with it. "Soul mates come in many forms," they had said at the soul mate workshop.

Now I was in Las Vegas with a magician, as the woman of his life. I wasn't even sure of it myself as I sat there in my Hawaiian slippers and my favorite red silk summer dress from Holland. I was holding Ravindu's hand at a poker table in the casino I knew from *Oceans Eleven*.

"When I squeeze your hand, close your eyes. When I squeeze again, open them," he said.

Every time I opened my eyes, hundred and thousands were falling in his lap. He was winning every time. "It works," he said.

Everybody knew him there: the restaurant owner, the manager of the casino, the pianist. "Christel is from *Holland*," he would say. The eyes of the manager lit up or the pianist would play a song for me.

"But wait," I said, as he introduced me to all the groupies. Twenty families had moved with him—from Philadelphia to New York, from Los Angeles to Chicago—just to be in his presence. He introduced me to his ex-wife and children. "This is my new love, and there will never be another one again."

"But wait," I said. I felt my life drifting away from that initial pull.

I was so far away from my call, my call for Hawaii, and I had now landed in the opposite of it: the dry desert, or, even worse, a casino. Then I started to hear hear it, very faint at first, the whisper, and it got louder every day. I ignored it at first. It only said one word. And I didn't know what it meant. It said: "Mesmerized."

It took me three days to find out what that meant. I asked a random construction guy, his orange safety helmet bobbing as he walked down the street. "Hypnotized," he said.

I thought I had stepped out of Ravindu's influence until a group of students gathered around Shen and me at the Qigong retreat. Shen started to wave his hand in front of my eyes, around my head, and then in front of my belly, grunting and yelling, "Ha!"

I felt it. It fell away around me. I stepped out of a dream, a real dream, instantly regaining my senses, my smell, and my hearing. The colors were coming back. I stepped forward and *had* to look back. I expected to see what I had stepped out of—a cloud feeling so real, so tangible, and so embedded that it had become part of me—but it wasn't there anymore. Right there and then, I vowed to never get distracted by a man again and never to lose my dantian. I was determined to go back to Hawaii to find out what that call for Hawaii really was. This time, I would not be letting any man distract or sidetrack me along the way.

Day 3: Lovemaking

UMBERTO'S HAND IS on my thigh, his compact hand and fingers caressing my white skin. The late afternoon sun plays over our bodies. Umberto doesn't have much attention for the rest of the apartment on this first visit. It's just a quick glance, as if he's afraid to see Lennard, who is on the other side of Honolulu. The elevator ride pushes us up, up, up, and we rush into my room, wanting to rip off our shorts and shirts as we fall upon the purple sheets.

Now he lifts up my skirt. *Touch me, touch me,* my body screams in excitement. *Let me feel your body. Let your body feel my body who it is.*

No time for admiration, slowly melting, or sweet words. Our breaths heavy and strong like beasts already. My hands moving up to his head, crawling through his thick, long black curls, my nails scratching the lines on his scalp, as if wanting to open them up. *Bladder meridian ... gallbladder meridian ... du mai or the governor meridian*: the places I got to know so well on other people's heads.

I want to tear them open on his head, one by one, until they bleed, from the beginning to the end, opening up all that information stored in there. Curling myself up against him and biting his neck, we move like wild snakes around each other. His amazingly dark skin, like velvet, wants to absorb me, wants to absorb my whiteness. Although my skin is tanned, I feel so white next to his deep, dark chocolate skin. Our lips find each other again, pressed together as juicy red veins united.

And there it happens. We transform into a whole community, a tribe, a world. We are making love to a world, and I can step into it. It is all around and through us. A world of exotic scents and faces is staring at me: dances, incantations, fire, and magic. I can just pull the worlds out of

Umberto, like long, colored veils wrapped inside of him for so long, now freely floating. And we can play with them, first opaque and impenetrable, but soon light and iridescent.

We float through these worlds while our bodies wrap wilder and wilder around each other. He penetrates me deeply. My body can't be more ripe and open. The being together seamlessly melts into times long ago. Groups of people are standing around us, next to my bed. Umberto's ancestral history is presented to me. Ancient times and spices, smells, and rituals appear like stars on the firmament. I can feel it in his strong arms. There is no need to explain. I understand the things he told me about: his childhood in Jayapura, his fascination with the invisible, the noble parts in him, wanting to live a simple, ordinary, and understandable life.

Never before have I experienced it in lovemaking except maybe with my first lover. Frans had a white, skinny, long body that rolled around mine. As we kissed, I looked into his big, watery blue eyes. We were launched into the cosmos—into solar systems where we looked like blue transparent beings. Everything was shiny and vibrating. I tried to find that access with other lovers, but it seemed impossible. Even with Ravindu, I could not find it. The love we shared seemed to be in just one reality. It stayed physical or, at most, poetic.

With Umberto, it is there again. It is not so much a world of light and vibration; it is more one of generations. It's like yellowed maps, old books, and dusty drawings that come alive as realms. There are so many faces on them. Eastern faces, whole tribes standing next to our bed in Waikiki. *What do you want? You who all look the same to me. What needs to be known? What is it that you carry? What do I see in this shadow?* They just stand there speechless, but it is clear they have a message. *But what is it?*

I wonder. And right next to this dark shadow, these many faces, my own history lights up, my white fairness. It is, as if I can hear my own independence and my own freedom screaming in my bones and blood. The Dutch motto: *Je maintaindrai, ik zal handhaven.* I will maintain. As independent and self-reliant as I feel myself, also so embedded and interwoven is the collective "we" around Umberto, his two island families, Hawaiian and Papuan.

His index finger trails over my back. I follow him with all that I am. Everything comes alive. We are naked together—reverberating, announcing the edge, and announcing the deepest melting possible. It all floods back, dribbles onto our skin, our muscles, our nerves, our veins, and the marrow in our bones. It is enriching all that we have absorbed from each other and falling into that one place of quiet magic and utter peace.

He laughs sheepishly as he looks me in the eye, almost embarrassed. All those eyes watching, all those worlds evoked around us, all that mystery revealed, and there is no more you and no more me.

The purple sheets slide on the ground around our sweaty bodies. The fresh mountain breeze enters through the little glass louvers. I turn my head toward Umberto and tell him that I will leave in three weeks for the Big Island. I will lead a Qigong retreat for ten days with Dutch guests.

"This is why I came to Hawaii in the first place. I want to share the way Hawaii called me with others and support them in the process of following their calling." I feel the swelling of the excitement in my own voice and sense how it is already separating us.

My words float freely in the room—, right through the intensity in the air from a minute ago, through the passion, through the worlds created—, but they are not landing in him. I wonder if he will he understand. I feel so incapable of conveying what I am doing to anybody really, but especially to him, to Umberto. He who is not about rising up, not about putting feet firmly on the ground, not about having a clear voice and opening his intervertebral space. I could talk about swimming with dolphins or climbing the snow-covered Mauna Kea or meeting goddess Pele in the active lava flow of the volcano, but then I would be missing the point. Then I would be missing that which is created—, the magic, the mana, the Qi, the serendipity,— that which rises, even above words and above common reason.

Umberto stares at the ceiling fan. "Wow, the Big Island," he mumbles.

I am relieved that I don't have to bridge the gap I have started feeling. I study his face; little pearls of sweat drip from his forehead. I see him swallow; his gaze is swirling with the fan. This is the second time he has reacted strangely after hearing the name of the Big Island.

I touch his dark brown leg with my white fingers. He turns his face toward me, anxiety appearing in his eyes. With a hoarse voice, he asks if I will come back.

The many bonds we created are already so palpable, and they are trying to tie us together forever. Any sexual connection gives the illusion of never separating again.

"Yes, for sure. I will come back to Honolulu. After ten days."

Aumakua

TWO AND A half years earlier, in May 2002, I was on my first trip to Hawaii and spending my very first day there. Standing in Kealakekua Bay on the black, round lava rocks and looking out to the ocean, my body moans with pleasure. When I enter the water, I am surprised by the softness of its warm, soft embrace. Finally, I can swim freely in the ocean.

I have always been a good swimmer. I was a champion back home, and I can show it off to this vast body of water. Here in Kealakekua Bay, "the pathway of the Gods," I am wearing my new rainbow swimsuit, ready to meet the dolphins. Amazed, sucked in by the blueness, I swim farther and farther away from the shore. I don't see fish, seaweed, or coral—just an endless stretch of clear blue water, an ocean bed of white sand, and me.

I curl my body up and dive straight down, my arms next to my body like a mermaid, enjoying my new freedom. I let go of all the clients I had to see to get here and feel the flatness of Holland draining out of me, the exhaustion of the flight. I burst out laughing in my snorkel a few times, wishing my friends, twelve time zones away, could see me on my first day in Hawaii.

When I finally lift my head above the water and move my mask up my forehead, I feel fear. The black shoreline appears so tiny. The white monument to Captain Cook on the bare brown escarpment to the right appears so close. I had swam about a mile already. The ocean is feeling so much bigger now, overwhelming me. My small body is starting to lose strength. My arms feel heavy now.

Concentrating, I listen to my own breath hardening. I try not to get tired while swimming back to shore. When I peer down to the ocean floor, it is there. It's like a shadow at first—immobile on the white, sandy bottom.

Ten feet beneath me, longer than the length of a car. A shark. I can see it, and I can hear it. It makes a deep, wide rumbling sound. It's like an earthquake but more focused. It is the deepest, most overwhelming sound I have ever heard, a vibration of utter power. Instead of making me afraid, it stirs a primeval power in me, in my gut, in my flesh, in my bones, in every part of my being. I am the supreme queen of the ocean. I feel like we have the same power. We are only separated by respect. Absolute respect.

For minutes, we just look at each other. Motionless. Not wanting to let go of this moment. I am floating on the surface, feeling the animal presence beaming out of the shark. It is time to return to my humanness, my green towel on the stones, and my rental car on the shore. Gracefully moving my new blue fins up and down, I feel the separation taking place in awe and wonder. I am like a baby moving away from its mother, moving farther and farther away.

The friendly gurgling of water in my ears is changing to a drumbeat. The drumbeat is creating a strong undertone, beating louder and louder in my ears. My skin feels too thin, and my flesh feels too exposed. Every inch of my body enters high alert. There is no connection left with the shark. The respect has turned into fear. It squeezes my throat. It is released from the deepest fleshly caves of my pelvis.

The water has become alien, my enemy. I am in his territory, and he can devour me at any moment. My body is unable to move—as if not knowing how to obey. Then adrenaline releases, racing through my body, boosting every part to swim. I swim for my life as I feel the end so close in his presence behind me. When I finally reach the shore, the tiny waves have become monsters. They crash on the rocks and spit me out. I am scraped all over. For minutes, I am like a beached whale, shaking and panting for what feels like hours. Opening my eyes, I see two legs and two brown feet.

"Aloha," a friendly voice says. A dark-skinned man kneels down next to me. "Are you okay?"

"Yes." I try to sit up on the uncomfortable rocks to regain my composure. Wondering what I look like, scratches all over and still feeling the adrenalin rush pulsing, the word *aloha* still bouncing back and forth in me, resonating, creating a pleasant, exotic feel.

I am unable to find words. I look at the softest brown eyes. His face is of a culture I don't know yet—Hawaiian. A round complexion, deep brown eyes, short fingers, thick, wavy black hair beautifully draped over his shoulders. In this moment, my dreams and visions collide. It's as if they had come a few airplanes later.

I point at the water. "Shark," I say, feeling too exhausted to say anything else.

He smiles. "The shark is your aumakua." And then he walks away, disappearing between the shrubs and trees. No explanation, no further introduction, nothing.

My what? Aumakua?

Day 5: The Fin Slicing

ALONG THE EDGE of Waikiki at Sans Souci Beach, there is a secluded corner just beyond the view of the usual tourists. We see a shady stone ledge, and Umberto climbs on, his bare feet ambling over the black lava stones. We sit down, and he gives me a tangerine. It dazzles against his dark velvet skin; he isn't wearing a shirt. I push my thumbnail into the rind, and a spray of juice hits my eye. I wonder where he got them. Juice drips freely on his bare thighs as he bites into his tangerine—skin and all. His eyes are wide, and he groans softly. When I place a piece of tangerine in my own mouth, I wince from the sourness. He smiles and spits the seeds across the stones into the ocean. Then he laughs; his dark velvet belly is shaking.

"Look!" Umberto freezes, concentrating, and points his short finger toward the ocean. "Look! A shark! There!"

Right at the end of the swimming area, around the blue buoy, I see a short black fin swirling around. It is definitely not the friendly round fin of a dolphin that I've gotten to know so well. Dolphin fins usually come in groups, but this one is sharp, cutting straight through the water, making sudden moves in different directions. The only two swimmers in the water are rolling about and laughing safely in the beach surf, far from the shark.

I can't help but look at Umberto's face, peering into the distance. He is squeezing his eyes, creating little wrinkles I hadn't noticed before, and I wonder for the second time if he needs glasses. His body seems frozen, now hard, and impenetrable, though it was soft and juicy a minute ago. The velvet glow has given way to a metal shine, like I have seen a few times now; his shape shifting. Uncomfortably, I move an inch further away from him. My body feels so round and soft and Dutch next to his.

His energy change is almost audible. "My father's ancestors' spirit is a shark," he says, stern and short without mumbling. Is it his ancestors who are actually speaking to me now?

"Is it like the aumakua for the Hawaiians?" I ask, hesitating, afraid to disturb his trance. The moment reminds me of my first encounter with a shark and the words from the Hawaiian that followed: "The shark is your aumakua."

"Yes, Papuans believe in ancestral spirits too. They can inhabit the bodies of sharks or lizards or birds. My grandfather was able to collect and redirect the mana, the energy of the shark."

"For what?" I ask.

He turns his head toward me suspiciously. His eyes are small—the eyes of a predator. I shiver, and my body tightens.

"To heal or for magic." His lips soften slightly. His eyes widen, and his pupils float again in endless white. "He could only summon those powers at night. He used shark teeth as an amulet. Seeing a shark means that my ancestors are trying to speak." He points at the black shape moving in the water.

"I know," I say softly. My eyes watch as the fin comes a little closer, almost straight toward us. In a sudden move, it turns around. My belly starts to tingle. I've felt this strange excitement a few times now. I'm strong and safe with my legs on the rocks and not in the water, but I feel an incredible magnetic urge to be with the shark. I feel I am being held in the precise balance between utter power and extreme fear.

"What do you mean?" Umberto mumbles, a little condescending.

I smile and jump up. "Come on. Let's go home." I point at the disappearing fin in the distance while my other hand pulls his arm.

It is hot when we arrive back in my little room. The tiny square of my skin barely touched by his finger on the bottom of my spine, next to my sacrum, is electric. The hair stands up. It feels like the shark is still with us—right here, right now. *More, yes, give me more please.*

Umberto's energetic tendrils reach so deep inside of me, awakening those long-forgotten places. *Please let me be intimate with all your deepest wishes and your deepest longing. Show yourself to me. Like we can only allow ourselves in our skin touching skin.*

We roll on and over each other, every limb embracing. We are ready for complete destruction or extreme transcendence. All my senses are caressed;

wave after wave runs through my skin. *I am making love to the shark in you. The predator, your teeth devouring every part of me. The dorsal fin still slicing the surface. Your metal-like erection against the softness of my inside.*

And now, as I feel his warm come, I know the agreement we made once before—long ago in a magical realm. As children of the same blood, we would remain true to one another, no matter how long the journey, no matter what the challenge, no matter how far apart we strayed. Yet we would never really live together.

Delog

IN 1993, I was twenty-four. I spent seven weeks in Dharamsala, the Tibetan community in north India, after a failed relationship brought me to India in the first place. Arriving in Dharamsala was a delight after busy Delhi. I decided to stay there—alone—for the rest of my time.

The first day there, I met Jhampa Khelsang in the library of the monastery. He was a doctor in Tibetan medicine and astrology. When I told him I was studying Chinese medicine, he said, "Because Tibetan medicine is the mother of all medicine, I think you should know about the source of it." He was convinced that it was important for me to learn and for him to teach me.

There was just a picture of the Dalai Lama on the wall and two little windows with small curtains in a Tibetan motif. And outside there was the rain, the constant pouring monsoon rain on the tin roof of the little green house next to the big monastery. Every afternoon at two o'clock, I would walk up the steep hill in the rain and sit across from this little Tibetan man on the bed in the simple room where he lived with his sister.

He would unwrap the Tibetan tantras, sacred medicine texts, from an orange cloth with his delicate fingers and arrange them between us on a green wool blanket. The smell of Tibetan incense filled the room. Traditional Tibetan butter tea warmed on the stove for afterward.

"Here, give me your pulse first," he commanded me each day.

I reached my left palm toward him as he gently laid his three fingers on my pulse. First, the index finger—closest to my wrist—reached for my heart. Then the middle finger on the second position with a little more pressure to read the liver and gallbladder. His ring finger reached for the deepest position, my kidneys, the deep waters. With each finger, I sensed him descending into deeper layers of me, precisely navigating through all there was to feel. Never before had my pulse been taken so carefully, with so much depth and attention.

In the many Chinese medicine classes, it was always more a mechanical format, more about the status of empty and full, hot and cold. It was never about the deep connection, knowing past and future. Jhampa's focus was now on the deep position, moving his ring finger slightly around, searching. I always wondered what he was looking for. He gazed at the wooden floor, his eyes moving back and forth from right to left as if he were reading words rapidly from a book.

In deep concentration, I felt my breath deepening with his. I was descending with him. I knew it was not about the physical—not the way my kidneys do their work—but about the deep wisdom stored in them. The wisdom that is stored in my bones connects me to my ancestry and the deep still timelessness, which I am born for in the first place. It reveals my unique path, my challenges, my distractions, and the potential that is ultimately there. He would tilt his head a little more.

I knew he saw me. He was showing me who I am and which paths I could choose to take. He was so gentle, loving, and wise. There was never a need to utter a word about it.

He would smile and squeeze my arm slightly before he pulled his hand away. He would take a deep breath and recite long, mumbling words for an hour and a half, words I couldn't make sense of. He was reciting the tantras in Tibetan and moving his head rhythmically up and down. "A sacred transmission, your consciousness will get it anyway," he would say.

He would translate it for me in English afterward, although it was the least important part according to him. It was about Tibetan pulse diagnoses; so different from the pulse diagnoses I had learned in Chinese medicine. That diagnosis merely focused on the organs and their functions, while the mix from wind, phlegm, and bile could diagnose whole spiritual stories in the Tibetan pulse.

And this is where I heard the word *delog* for the first time.

He had just finished explaining how to diagnose the pulse of someone who is dying. He told me how to predict the death of somebody at a great distance and how to feel someone's impending death in a pulse: in the harshness, the tempo, the squeezing out the last vestiges of the life force.

He talked about the desperate attempt of blood to hold on to the veins of life, the division of that which was normally so interwoven. I could feel the tearing out of memories, of lessons lived, of food eaten, of flesh growing, while spirit was leaving the body. I could feel the desperation of the soul wanting to leave it all; the way he pictured it for me made it so palpable. I remember just trying to understand what he was saying and wondering if I would ever be able to feel the pulse that way myself. He changed the subject and started talking about Tibetan women who die, stay dead for a few days, and then come back and give reports from the other side. They consciously leave their bodies, accompanied by a guide.

"What did you say? Delog?"

"Yes, it literally means 'returned from death' in Tibetan."

Fascinated, I looked at his face, covered with fine lines. He gestured how her body is carefully watched over by others. The body doesn't decompose. There are no vital signs, no breath, no pulse, and no warmth for about five days.

"Like, er ... really dead?" Saying it out loud felt ridiculous. You are either dead or not dead—not just a little bit dead or temporarily dead.

He nodded and told me in his broken English it would be announced weeks before, in dreams or meditations, so others could meditate alongside her. The delog is a messenger, bringing questions from the community to the other side to be able to report, to witness, bringing back important messages for family and the whole community, and getting a deeper understanding of death and dying. They roam around in the afterlife.

Bardo, the Tibetans call it, "the in- between state." Bardo is the place where every desire, every pain, every wish, every power, and all the attachments to earth are experienced. It is the place of the great distraction. It is, where your soul lets go of the old attachments to earth and your old identity, on your way to the pure, the crystalline realms.

Jhampa said that we all spend forty-nine days in Bardo—from the moment we leave our bodies at death until the moment we enter our new lives or the pure realms.

One moment, a delog encounters family and friends who have passed on. The next moment, she might endure the most hideous torments of hell. She might meet virtuous persons on their way to a pure realm or find herself in God's realm. They seem like ordinary people in their daily lives, yet the experience is a sign of great realization. They have always had a background of great spiritual achievements in a past life or through their lineage.

"Always women?" I asked.

Jhampa paused, and his expression changed. I felt strange for a moment. It was as if he could see so much more. He answered that it was usually women because of different energetics.

"But it is not impossible for men," he added. His eyes were resting in mine, and I sensed him penetrating a veil in me. It was like he was able to look straight into my future. A strange tension appeared in my gut. The scent of the butter tea suddenly swirled strongly through the room. I heard children's voices yelling from the nearby school. The rain stopped.

I knew he knew so much more than I was comfortable with—just like when he did my astrological chart and came up with some strange details. Some that were really right on, and others were really peculiar. He told me about the mole on my right upper thigh, which initially sounded like such an unimportant detail, but I became obsessed with it. Did he really see it? Had he gazed under my skirt? What would that little mole be a sign of?

Despite the discomfort, I was intrigued by the phenomenon of delogs. I could not stop asking questions. I wondered why we in the Western world never heard about it. Near-death experiences always seem to happen to somebody. It never seemed like a conscious choice—let alone coming back from death after a few days. And it all happens with a full awareness, from the one who dies as well as the ones surrounding her.

His sister walked in with a basket of groceries, leaving the door open and letting in the first rays of sunlight I had seen for days.

Djawa looked at us, not hiding her shyness as she had before. I could feel her sensing the subject and my interest in it even though her English was very poor. Her eyes opened wide.

When I smiled back at her, she looked away, grabbed two little bowls, and took the tea off the stove. The two of us looked silently at the liquid with the delicious creamy taste pouring into the cups. The scent of butter tea was now strongly filling the room.

"So, how do they die?" I asked.

Jhampa said, "They just get sick, usually very suddenly, without any clear cause. They fall into a coma, often overnight. Or they have a very high fever, a liver or kidney failure, cancer, or poisoning. It can be anything. Medicines usually don't help; they just aggravate it. Then after the delogs die and return from death, everything appears to be normal. Usually their ailments have been cured miraculously. Because they get a deep insight as to how illness is created in the first place, it is all about the spirit, Christel."

That grabbed my attention even more. I held my breath. His words felt so true, yet so the opposite of everything modern medicine tells us, even what I had learned from Chinese medicine. Going through these realms at this high pace gives very clear responses in the body. A lot of clearing takes place. The body instantly heals, and the delog gets to see how the illusion of the illness has come into being. By having the spiritual clearing, the body just follows. They usually come back perfectly fine. Sometimes the people watching over the body see subtle changes in it, depending what she is going through.

For a moment, I tried to imagine myself sitting next to a dead body— the soul still tethered to it, a cold stiff body, not breathing, no beating heart, a body that science would say will never be able to function again, nothing to see that would signal the return. I felt slightly nauseous.

Djawa was now sitting on the bed wearing a colorful wool top. Something in her eyes revealed familiarity with the subject, and it gave me chills. For a moment, I wondered if I should ask her if she has had an experience like this. I realized the absurdity of the question. Besides, she probably wouldn't even understand my words.

Jhampa seemed in a meditative state.

The simple room with the low roof all of a sudden felt full—as if it had become filled with all the delogs that ever were. My questions faded as I felt Djawa's fingers against mine, reaching out the warm tea to me. The cup held so much more than tea, herbs, and butter.

It was dark when I stepped outside.

Day 7: Diamond Head

IT IS HOT, and the dark tunnel into the crater has a welcoming, cold breeze. It has taken us an hour to finally reach Diamond Head, the big volcanic crater next to Waikiki. Umberto and I pause to cool off after the long walk, sitting at the edge of the tunnel with our backs against the wall and our knees pulled up. We hear echoes of excited children all around us. Families are entering and exiting the tunnel.

It is noon, and the bright light on the other side seems overwhelming.

"I miss Jayapura," Umberto starts. "It is so beautiful there, just like Hawaii, only less people. And there is magic … a lot of magic."

I tell him that the Indonesians in Holland call it *de Stille Kracht,* which means something like "the silent force."

He nods pensively.

I look at the lines of the sharp profile of his face and the bright light behind it. I could make a paper cutting out of it. I love to listen to Umberto's stories. They are so exotic and so far away from where I came from. He represents something about my urge to be in Hawaii, but I cannot quite figure out what.

"Once I was with my grandfather in the forest in Jayapura, the forest that I always loved to go to. It is more tropical than Hawaii, a real rainforest; the trees almost seem alive. We walked the usual trail, and all of a sudden, this tree appeared in the middle of the road. It just appeared instantaneously, huge and impossible to go around. An unusual tree—like I had never seen before. Big roots were sticking in the ground everywhere."

"Then what?" I start to feel a little chilly, and I cross my arms around my legs. The cool tunnel is now losing its appeal.

Umberto is still looking in front of him. "He used a spell. The tree

41

just started to crumble and died right in front of us in a couple of seconds. It was still there, but it fell down and was brown and dead. We could just step over it. I was really scared. I even peed in my pants."

I hold my breath, letting Umberto's words enter me. I think of the ease with which he used the word *spell*, the familiarity even, despite the fact that he was scared. I involuntary burst out laughing. "You peed in your pants?" My laugh echoes in the tunnel, covering up the squeeze of fear released of the middle of my adrenals. *Spell? Spell.* It bounces back and forth in my head.

The cold is creeping through my skin. It freezes me and immobilizes me, lingering in my mind. I see images of black magic, old family feuds, magic potions, scary practices, and abuses of power. Umberto says he has inherited these same powers; it has been in his family a long time. It was used to protect the village and other things. Umberto is Papuan, and it appears he is into spells. He says he never learned to use those powers, magic words, or rituals, but strange things have happened.

"One time a cousin of mine, she was a schoolteacher, died really young. Nobody knew why, and you know what? Just before they were going to close her coffin, she woke up! I saw it with my own eyes. She opened her eyes, and after an hour, she stepped right out of the coffin."

"What?" I stand up. Stretching my legs feels good.
"Yeah, the strange thing is that her body didn't seem to disintegrate. It just kept on being fresh. It was almost as if she was sleeping. Her skin was shiny and flawless. It is a sign of these forces when people die that their body remains intact. There can be all kind of reasons for her death: revenge, a fight, an old family feud, or power over an unwilling lover." He slowly pulls himself up.

My body hair stands up like a scared cat. The mumbled words are echoing in my mind. He said it with so little emotion, which makes it so scary.

For a moment, I want to run away. This is the first time I am threatened by his words. I want to run back out of the tunnel, out of the shadow, out of Diamond Head, out of this neighborhood, away from him. Even away from this island, away from Waikiki, away from the unknown water. Unwilling lover? What if that unwilling lover is me? I want to go back to Holland. Everything is flat and clear there. There are no mysterious corners, strange trees, or powers. I want to go back to Holland and just eat a *boterham met pindakaas*, a sandwich with peanut butter, licorice, and chocolate sprinkles. I want to have nothing to do with spells or magic powers that manipulate reality. I want to be with my husband. Lennard can make me laugh about anything. I want to go back to the Big Island—to the house I am housesitting in Kealakekua Bay—and feel the sunshine on my skin. I want to swim with the dolphins and be true to that which brought me here in the first place, that call for Hawaii.

He smiles, grabs my hand, and pulls me into the crater. The sun is brutal. It's a colossal surreal landscape. There is no wind or shade—just a big, flat yellow sandy surface and Japanese tourists with the same hats, cameras, and long-sleeved jackets.

I blink a few times to get used to the overwhelming light. The sun feels good on my skin, somehow making me feel stronger. I breathe in the warm air, realizing that nothing can happen to me. I am not going let my power be stolen anymore. I had promised Dr. Shen. "It is all up to you," Shen said. I stretch my neck, feel my vertebrae open up, and shake out my hands for a moment. *Yes, it is all up to me.* I walk next to Umberto on the gravel path that winds up to the top of the crater. With each step, I can feel my power coming back more. I feel taller and taller.

"Yeah, sometimes people just become crazy and lose their minds," says Umberto. "I have seen that too. One guy was a friend of mine. Samson was perfectly normal one day and became totally crazy the next. He just started yelling in the middle of a crowd, and he never got out of it. Nobody was able to communicate with him or make any sense of what he was shouting ever again."

"It sounds so negative," I say. I try to stretch my neck in different directions.

"My grandfather said it is not so much negative or positive. It is just what it is. And it serves a purpose. He would say that when there is a connection made to something or somebody, the influence stays—however big the distance is."

The little stones crackle beneath our slippers as we slowly start to ascend to the lookout above Diamond Head. Our fingers are hooked around each other as he walks in front of me. I see the cracks on his heel.

The pink flesh curls around his feet. The palms of his feet and hands are the only places where he is not covered with dark velvet skin.

"The only thing that helps is praying," he tells me.

"What did you just say?"

He turns around and looks at me, sweat pearling on his forehead. "The only thing that helps is praying. It's the only way to get rid of the forces."

"Oh." I watch him turn his back toward me again. *Praying? What do you mean by praying? Praying like in a church? Begging God for help?*

A few stones tumble down in front of me. As they roll down the path, my feet slip from under me. I can't catch my balance, and I try to grab the railing.

"Watch out!" he says, but it is already too late. I am sliding down the hot, dry yellow gravel. As I fall, I see a few glistening stones in front of me. *What do you mean by praying?* The question for Umberto is still with me, but I feel too far away to voice it. On my belly, I repeat it softly to myself.

Little dust clouds curl up all around. British sailors who mistook the glistening stones for diamonds named it Diamond Head. I grab a little stone and roll it through my fingers. I see the shiny little glitters. "Diamonds," I say as I scan my body for pain. I have scratched knees, a hurt elbow, and a bruised right leg. I don't want to stand up. I don't want Umberto's help to stand up. I don't want to examine this sensitive subject that he has mentioned a few times now: the church and praying.

A young couple behind us wants to pass by, and I get up reluctantly.

In silence, we continue up the path, which has now become stairs with a more substantial handrail. Umberto's words swirl through my mind.

Of all the Indonesian islands, Irian Jaya or West Papua stands out the most to me. Involuntarily, I see that map appearing in front of me. My astrocartography map had every aspect of my astrological chart projected on the globe. Grace, my friend and an astrologer, showed me the map after she explained my natal chart. I looked at the blue, red, green, black, and yellow lines that ran straight up and straight down all over the planet. It showed how alternative aspects of existence are more prevalent in various areas of the world—some more and some less favorable.

"During certain periods of your life, it can be very good to be in a specific place," she said.

I saw a line running through Hawaii. A black line running straight through West Papua caught my attention.

"What is that line, Grace?" I asked.

"Oh, that is not such a pleasant one." She started laughing out loud, but then she looked at me seriously over her red reading glasses. "Chiron represents the wound. It's the wound that doesn't need to be fixed or cured or gotten rid of like traditional medicine or psychology says. Instead Chiron takes you on a journey through your darkness, seeking light, in search of the gift in the wound," she said mysteriously, lifting her eyebrows as she looked at me.

Day 10: Scents

"MAN, YOU SHOULD be a magician, a fire dancer, a professional surfer, or have a chocolate farm just like your dad," I say impatiently. My feet want to go in a faster pace as we are trailing along Kalakaua, the road right next to the ocean. We are passing groups of Japanese tourists and joggers and families smelling like sunscreen and surfer girls and boys with big boards crossing our path, ready to jump on the waves. I walk in front of him. "But working in a county office? I just cannot believe it."

I cannot help but thinking about our lovemaking last night. It happened again. Those faces, the appearances, that strange magical world. It was so animalistic, so raw, and so exotic. Our skin melted together, and this man works in an office?

We now enter Kapiolani Park, a beautiful park with old big trees and a zoo in the middle. I smell the freshly mown grass and point to the little field to the left. "That is where I teach Qigong every Friday morning to Lennard and a few friends."

He asks me to show him, and I throw off my slippers and step on the grass. I put my feet parallel to each other, shoulder width apart, stretch my toes, and pull in my pelvic muscles. I relax my shoulders, pull in my chin, and stretch my neck. I close my eyes for a moment. As I inhale the smell of the nearby plumeria tree, I feel my body relax.

"Look, this is the wuxi stance. It is the basic posture in which you activate your dantian, which initiates spontaneous movements in your body. The dantian is an energy center in your lower belly." I point to a flower print on my dress. "It is like a second brain that knows exactly where there is tension in the body. And given the right encouragement, it will try to correct it. At the same time, it opens the intervertebral spaces. Look, you know gravity, right?"

He nods.

"Well there is also something like the opposite of gravity. The pushing force of the earth is like a vibration. That is what makes things grow. This force in everything is even much more than that. Shen, my teacher, says the older you get, the more gravity gets a hold on you. 'It pulls you to your grave,' he says sarcastically. When you allow yourself to stretch and relax your muscles, this force starts to flow." My arms start to shake, and my body starts to wiggle slightly.

Umberto laughs at me.

"You want to try? People really become taller when they practice."

"No, I like gravity," he lies down on the grass with his hands supporting his head.

Umberto's mouth is all stretched out. All of his teeth are visible, his eyes are closed, and tears are flowing out of the corners. There is grass in his hair; he looks like a child laughing at a dirty joke and rolling around. He started laughing when I told him about Lama Fahai, Shen's teacher, an acupuncturist who would spit acupuncture needles from his mouth right into his patients. When I started telling him that I believe in curing yourself through Qigong, or healthy information transmission, or even choice—rather than through regular medicine or acupuncture—he started to laugh even louder.

"You mean, there is a choice? When you are sick? When you have a headache, a sore back, or bad stomach? You think there is a choice?" He laughs in disbelief, rolling over to his back and pulling his arms around his shaking belly as if the laughter is killing him. I have seen him do that a few times now.

How do I end up with this guy who has such a different perspective on life? *What am I doing with you?* I look at his wide blue jeans and his white shirt streaked green from the cut grass.

When Umberto stops for a moment to catch his breath, I try to explain how I once had a whiplash after a car accident. I couldn't move my head for a few days. My neck felt broken, and I had a terrible headache. I thought my life was over, but Shen started pulling on my ring finger. I immediately felt a click in my neck. Instantly, the pain flushed out of my head. A few minutes later, I couldn't even imagine how much I had suffered. Shen just took the unhealthy information out, which I could have done myself through Qigong.

Umberto stops laughing and rolls on his side, his red eyes still wet from tears. "Really?" he says, curling his lip.

"Yeah. It is all about healthy information transmission. Come on. Let's continue walking." I start to feel impatient with him.

"I would love to get some of that healthy information transmission of yours," he says as he gets up behind me and kisses my neck.

Kapiolani Park has a lot of activity and parties on weekends, but on a Tuesday, it is almost empty. I point at a little table under a tree what seems to be a display. A man is sitting motionless on a chair behind it.

"What a blodo," Umberto mumbles. Blodo? What kind of word is that? I look Umberto in the eyes, but he just shakes his head.

As we come closer to the little table, we see the display of about a hundred little brown bottles with liquid in them. A sky blue cloth is underneath them. The short man behind the table doesn't greet us.

Umberto tugs at my dress, pulling me in another direction.

"No, wait." I walk straight toward the table. "Hello," I say as I stand in front of the display. We are the only ones there; there is nobody in the park around us.

I look him straight in his eye, a white cloud covers his pupils. He is blind. He stretches out his hand toward me, and I grab it. I feel an instant connection with this white-haired man. I feel Umberto's resistance a few feet behind me. I hold the old man's hand longer than usual in a handshake, and I can feel him scanning me.

I turn to Umberto and point at my eyes.

"Oh." He nods, apparently irritated that we are not leaving. "What a blodo," he whispers.

I tilt my head for a moment, lifting up my both hands.

"What do you mean by, blodo?"

The man interrupts before Umberto answers. "Hello, my name is Francesco. I have these essential oils from all these flowers. I made them myself." The blind man seems so small on the chair and almost looks like he is from another world.

"I am Christel, and this is Umberto." I point to Umberto and smile as I realize he cannot see my gesture.

"Nice to meet you, Christel and Umberto." He smiles for a moment and stretches out his fingers as if he is ready to play the piano for us. "Would you like to smell the essences I made?"

He takes a little bottle out of the wooden holder, opens it, and holds it up, smelling it first himself. "Mm, here you try, Umberto. That is tuberose."

"I know. That is my mother's favorite smell," Umberto says with the most excitement in his voice I have heard for days. As he smells the little bottle, a smile appears on the man's face. It's like he knows so much more than we suspect. Umberto lifts his eyebrows all the way up, almost pushing his eyes out of the sockets.

I chuckle at the sight of it.

Francesco opens another little bottle and holds it out to Umberto.

"Plumeria, my favorite," Umberto yells.

The blind man is scanning the little bottles with his fingers, smiling mysteriously, and nodding in my direction. There must be at least eighty different scents. The bottles all look the same. They don't even seem to have labels. I open my mouth in amazement.

His long, sensitive fingers touch the little bottles, scanning each one as if he can smell them with his fingers. "Here." He takes a little bottle, opens it, and lets me smell it. I cannot smell anything. The strong smell of plumeria from Umberto's bottle still lingers in my nostrils. When I tell the old man, he bends down and opens a deep, round, wooden box. It is too dark to see what is inside. Surprised, I inhale the smell of coffee. "Coffee beans clear the receptors from the smell they were holding," he explains.

I look at the shiny, yellowish skin on his forearm as he sticks out the same bottle again. It is a delightful aroma, but I do not recognize the smell.

"It is night-blooming jasmine." He pauses for a moment. "I thought you might like it."

Day 14: Protection

AGED AND GRUBBY, the yellowed hallway of the King Kamehameha apartment building is featureless except for the entrance gate and the door to the upstairs elevator. The metal gate clangs like a rusty church bell in the dreary hallway, echoing my feelings for Umberto. *Don't do it. Don't do it,* My internal voice is unrelenting and loud. The gate precisely determines the boundary between him and me.

At first, I can only see the silhouette, in which he appears so stooped. Drooping shoulders, turned out flat feet, as if no support was ever given to them, in slippers that are too big. Sharp behind him the bright blue sky and the dazzling Honolulu sun. Then I come a few steps closer, and the dark face becomes more pronounced. *Who are you? Who is this man who has dropped so randomly into my life? Who has no big dreams or juicy desire to expand? Who has no determination to reach out into the world like I do? Is it just sexual lust? Is it the addiction to getting lost together or getting lost in exotic worlds and wanting to forget about our separate lives?* His body becomes a shadow that I want to pull through the bars of the gate—like dark liquid chocolate—and swallow my fair skin whole with his darkness. I know that he can make the metal wall just an illusion.

My eyes meet his eyes, the only contrast in the dark figure. Bulged eyes, dark currants in endless milk. *Why do I let you in? Why do I open the gate to my life? My heart? My body?* My hand is resting on the doorknob. In a split second, I can see it clearly. I can hear the metal of the gate melting and transforming into golden cogs that turn vast wheels. The wheels so much bigger than me. Two big wheels perfectly come together, turn around each other, and hit at precisely one point. It is just one tiny moment in time, and then…the wheel turns.

My body screams for more time. I focus on the angular pattern of the gate. He is a blur behind it. I grab the doorknob resolutely and turn it. In me, it fades. I am not able to feel it anymore.

He is inside.

"Hi," he says bashful as he shuffles in.

***

"Why do you always act so weird when I mention the Big Island? You always seem to want to look away, change the subject, or roll your eyes. Is it because you are afraid that I am going to leave you, that my future is waiting for me there?" We are sitting on my new red bedspread that I bought today with Lennard at Macy's. I love the rich feel of it. I slide my hand over it to feel the soft, silky texture. I follow the embroidered flowers with my fingers. Uncomfortably, he puts one knee over the other.

"No," he says shortly, shaking his head and staring down.

My red nails match the bedspread. I stretch out my feet in front of me. "So?"

I see him tremble for a moment. It is as if an electrical current is running through his body. Then, as if in a trance, it all comes out of him.

"My mother is Hawaiian. She was born on the Big Island, close to the volcano on the Hilo side of the island. That is where she was raised in the Hawaiian culture. She is from Ali'i ancestry, meaning a royal Hawaiian lineage. When I was born, as the eldest, my parents went back to her native soil. She asked a kahuna to put protection around me to protect that Ali'i energy, and that is what he did. I still remember how the kahuna did a ceremony, with ti leaves, seawater, drumming, and singing. I was nine years old. Since then, there is this … curse around me. When I go to the Big Island, I become very sick. I want to leave as soon as possible. I get sick, and everything seems to be against me. Life is impossible for me there. A few times, the whole family had to leave the island because of me."

Protection? You would expect that when they put a protection around you that you are at least welcome. I bend down to try to look him in the face. "And what about your brother and sister?"

"Nothing."

"And your mother? Has she experienced it too?"

"No."

"But what is it? What do you think it is?" I am starting to become impatient with his short answers. I push my hand against his faded blue shirt, feeling his strong upper arm. I want to feel the resistance in his muscle, but he is weak and collapsed.

"What are you going to do about it when I live on the Big Island?" I realize what a perfect solution it is for my ambivalent feelings. He cannot come to my island, and that makes our relationship impossible. I have clarity in all my doubts. *"Daarmee is de kous af,"* as we would say in Holland. No more explanation necessary.

"I dunno." He shakes his head. "Strong powers."

Day 20: Christmas

"MILK IN YOUR tea?"

I am naked, lounging against the cool tile of the kitchen counter. I am admiring Umberto's dark torso, wide and strong, as he uses his shirt for a towel, rubbing his dark armpits, around his neck, over his cheeks, making his shirt into a strap to dry his back. Sweat is still dripping from his forehead. He shakes his head vigorously when I ask him if he would like a real towel. The windows of Lennard's apartment have become obscured with steamy condensation, and colored dots from melted Christmas lights are visible in the distance. It is my first Christmas in Hawaii, and we have the apartment to ourselves. Lennard is on his way to New York, England, and Spain in his search for the perfect lover. His paperwork is abandoned and strewn all around us.

"Just a little milk," Umberto replies to my question, turning his body toward me, motioning with a pincer shape of his fingers. But inside of me I know he actually likes a lot of milk. Just like his ravenous appetite in the love we just shared. It's like a big blanket flooding us,— more then ever before. This sense of wanting to have it all, wanting to get it all out, and let it all come over us. We cannot get enough of each other, needing to get to the core of it, while the moment of separation is coming closer and closer.

Tomorrow, I fly to the Big Island for ten days. I will be on another island, in another world, far away. We want to savor it all and dive to the bottom of this strange, ravenous hunger for each other, which I have begun to accept—even though it doesn't make any sense. We've known each other for almost four weeks.

"Just a little," I repeat as I open the fridge, reach for the milk, and shake my head. It is like he doesn't dare to know what he really wants. It is

53

the same with Umberto's physical presence. He never wants to take up the whole bed, but always too small a slice and he always wants to disappear when he sees Lennard. He is unwilling to make a stand.

"Are you hungry?"

"Not for me—no Christmas dinner." He shrugs as I hand him the cup of tea. My stomach hardens involuntary when I hear the word *Christmas*. My parents must have put up their Christmas tree by now—always at the last minute—in the big front window. I think of the angel hair, the special lights like flowers, the little nativity, and the sheep with the three legs that would never be able to stand up. I think of the scent of the delicious meals my mother makes wafting throughout the house—the subtle bouillon prepared for days, the salmon appetizer, the ox tongue, the traditional family meal on my father's side—and the plates with blue decorations, the silverware with our family name inscribed, and the apple pie. I am far away from them. I am not even allowed to leave the country for a while. The heat is too hot, the sun is too bright, my body is too naked, and Umberto is so foreign compared to my parents.

The apartment feels way too far from the ground on the twelfth floor, but I tell myself that I will be able to submerge myself in nature again tomorrow. I will stick my feet into the cold snow on the Mauna Kea, crawl into caves at the Kilauea crater, see the inside of the earth flow out in the glowing hot lava, and go back to why I came here in the first place. Back to where the whisper told me to go to: the Big Island. I will only be back in Waikiki after that for a few more weeks, and then I will be gone from here forever.

I look at Umberto; he pensively strokes the soft channel that runs between his nose and his lips with his middle finger. It is the end of the governor meridian. I cannot help but reproduce the two names of the acupuncture points in my head: *"moat"* and underneath it *"foothills of joy"* They bring back life when somebody is drowning.

***

This sense of hurry is still with us as we rush to the ocean, down the elevator, out of the gate, and over the sidewalk. We are running and laughing with just towels wrapped around our bare bodies. We cut through a long line of Japanese visitors with cameras and shoes with socks. There is the little strip of bars and shops, neon lights yelling their wares, and hula dancers singing "White Christmas". Through the bright lights, we cross the warm asphalt of Kalakaua Avenue. We walk across the cool white sand and out toward the dam, ready to cool off in the dark gentle waves, white foam caressing the hard rocks. We seem invisible to others; we are the only ones out there.

His dark body is almost seamlessly merging with the dark water; only his white eyes are visible as he turns around. The soft water envelopes us, his strong arms embrace me, my legs tight around his body, he wades through the water bouncing me up and down as if were walking on the moon. I hear a little squeak in his breath. I love to be carried.

"Don't leave, please." He puts his tongue in my ear, giving me chicken skin from tip to toe. I sigh, wanting to get drunk from him again, overwhelmed and intoxicated, like a junkie.

Tomorrow, I can sort it all out—when my life belongs to me again. Now, I want to fill myself up once more. I want to gorge—just like I gorged myself on the one-meter long marshmallows my father invented. We had a whole mountain of them in our garage when I was young.

"I'll be back. I promise!"

Day 21: Tsunami

DRIPPING ALL OVER, he rushes out of the shower. It is the morning before I leave, and it is the one time I turn on the TV in all the weeks I have been living on Oahu with Lennard. "Tsunami in Indonesia" the newscaster alerts.

"Tsunami in Indonesia," I yell.

"Atjeh," Umberto says slowly. Water drips like tears out of his dark skin, making a wet spot on the white carpet. He is frozen to the ground as the disaster unfolds before our very eyes.

"We lived right there for a long time." He points his wet hand to the screen as "Atjeh" appears in big letters. He is holding back as if he is afraid to touch upon the horrible devastation.

The earth shook on the morning of Boxing Day. Deep beneath the ocean, the earth's tectonic pressure released violently, creating a gigantic wave, striking hard, taking hundreds of thousands of lives instantly, and sucking souls out of their bodies. The vast ocean has taken with no mercy. We watch hundreds of thousands of bodies dragged ruthlessly into death from the place Umberto had lived. The earthquake cracked open the world—taking all that was built, all that had grown, and all that was alive—and effortlessly washed it away.

It is so unreal to sit in Lennard's white apartment on the twelfth floor. The sun is blazing down, and everything is coming to a stop as we watch, in slow motion, all the images: houses gone, faces frightened, wailing, screeching, and howling. The room is filled with a strange silence while images and voices blast out of Lennard's new Sony widescreen.

Reporters appear, popping up in a hurry. CNN, BBC, and NBC have the common pictures of every disaster: the military, improvised hospitals, the wailings of lost, big-eyed children, whole houses almost instantly disappearing into raging rivers. For the first time in my life, the pictures become alive. It is not a distant, surreal picture that I can shut off with the remote, close my eyes to because it was too big to grasp, too big to understand, and too far away to feel real. I had learned to become numb to reports of shootings, bombs, earthquakes, and natural disasters.

Now, with my body still so enmeshed with him, still smelling of the sex we just had, the images gushing out of the screen are breathing and alive. For the first time, I feel there is no there and here. There is no separation between us; I am in the middle of it all. I wonder if it is my own heart beating in my ears, or if it is his: *a loud Kaboom. Kaboom. Kaboom.* It is louder and louder between us.

Is your family still living there? I want to ask him, but my words feel as if they would bounce senselessly off the walls. I bite my tongue.

"We ended up moving to Hawaii to be closer to my mother's family," Umberto whispers. He reads my mind and brings us somewhat back to our bodies. We are defeated as we look at the images and the remains.

"Have you been there recently?"

"Yeah. I was visiting my whole family last year. Some live in West Papua, but most of them in Atjeh."

I watch the words come out of his mouth and sense a dark cloud entering the room. All the love we squeezed in yesterday vanished. Only an intimate vulnerable feeling toward each other is left as we sit on the couch. The city outside has come alive again already. The sun shines relentlessly, and palm leaves wave in the wind.

"What time do you have to be at the airport?"

"The plane to Kona leaves at two." All at once, I do not feel like leaving at all. It has only been an hour since we heard the terrible news.

"I can go one day later."

Tears are running down his cheeks and dripping on the carpet. "No, you go. I will come with you to the airport and then go to my parents in Kailua. I will call a taxi right now."

The taxi has already arrived when I put the last clothes into my suitcase. We haven't been able to really say good-bye.

"Come here." I embrace Umberto and pull him tight against me. He is shaking. "We are coming!" I wave down to the taxi driver.

"What are you taking with you? Are you secretly moving?" Umberto carries my suitcase and big bag to the taxi.

"I have to be prepared for everything, snorkeling gear and warm clothes for the snow on top of the Mauna Kea. I think I will leave a few things on the Big Island so I don't have to take them back and forth."

"Which airline?" the taxi driver asks. On the dashboard, I see a piece of carpet with different little statues glued to it: a standing Buddha, a dragon, and a flag. It smells like incense.

"Hawaiian Airlines."

The radio is on, again we hear the message about the tsunami. I look at Umberto. He is lost in thought. A sweet Hawaiian song plays on the radio as if nothing ever happened. I take a deep sigh. Soon I will exchange the city for the Big Island—the place where I feel so at home. I let myself be taken away by the melody for a moment.

"I have to hurry." Umberto holds me, puts his hand on my heart and looks deep into my eyes. "I will miss you." He kisses me tenderly on my lips.

I enter the long row with tourists, sunburnt faces, and the smell of sweat and flowers. I glimpse back and see Umberto entering the bus. The cloud of the tsunami is still hanging on him.

It's strange. We've known each other only such a short time, yet he has become so much to me.

Day 22: Return

IT IS THE beginning of January, and my feelings for Umberto had dwindled while I was away. They faded to almost nothing as I submerged myself in the retreat for ten days.

Being on the Big Island always seems like being in another world, all my life in Honolulu seemed to have ceased to exist, even my connection with Umberto. But now that I am floating here with him on our backs, holding hands, our arms and legs stretched out like starfish, in the Waikiki ocean, under thousands of stars, things are different. We just made love twice—, once in my bedroom and once on top of the King Kamehameha building. We looked over the city while night was falling, and everything in me blasted wide open with everything in him. I am back to where I was before: fully infatuated.

I just returned from the Big Island this morning, still vibrating with the happy dolphins, the deep orange lava flow, the speaking waterfalls, and the white owl, the turtle, and shark. Umberto's many invisible energetic arms embrace me again, touching me and awakening all that he touched before. It is so easy to surrender again. Our flesh merges, but there is a feeling of innocence. We are in our magical world, and the dark blue ocean seamlessly merges with the dark blue sky. It looks like it is floating in the sparkling sky itself. My white body next to his dark one.

He kisses me softly on my cheek, waking me from my dream state. He smiles at me, I smile at him, and we look into each other's eyes. In this mundane gesture, we both sense a tableau of something bigger. We both somehow know what will inevitably follow.

"My parents are up there in an airplane." He points at a moving light, his face glimmering from the water sliding down like tears. "They left

Honolulu at eight o'clock. That could be them. They are on their way to Atjeh, visiting the family members who survived, even though they don't know yet who survived. They only got a message from Uncle Willy: 'Please come and help us."

When I look up, I see a tiny light between the other stars. "Really? They are going to Indonesia? Right to the devastation?" I had been without any news for almost two weeks, but in Lennard's apartment I was presented with it again: the big mess, the search for victims, the increasing death toll appearing on the screen in opaque numbers.

"They are going for two weeks or longer. So far, Uncle Willy is the only survivor they know about. I said good-bye to my parents this morning. It was so emotional. It is almost like I am losing them too. It is so hard to see them go, knowing the pain they will have to face."

"Wow." I feel inadequate. Words feel superfluous. We face each other with just our mouths above the water; our bodies hidden under the dark surface.

"We have twenty-one family members missing. I am sure they must be dead by now, but my parents speak of them with so much hope still. That is why they want to go—to search for survivors themselves. They cannot bear to wait, feeling so powerless from so far away."

I nod pensively, taking it all in.

Survivor... sur-vivors, *Overlevenden*. I translate inwardly in Dutch to make it more real. Survivors, the ones who lost everything but their lives. The word moves through my body like it has never done before, fear punching in my rib cage and powerlessness in my muscles. For one moment, I feel everyone who has ever survived a gigantic tragedy. I picture them stripped away from all that life had given, like a gigantic woven tapestry, pulled out till only the last little thread remained. With nothing to tether it to, everything disappears in one big void.

"Do you know all of the twenty-one people who died?"

"Yes, all of them. I saw them a year ago. Nobody in the family is alive anymore, I think."

Twenty-one? Twenty-one! It echoes in my mind.

I shake my head, imagining my family being washed away in an instant. The warm, dark water that was so enveloping at first now becoming the unknown water of Waikiki, so dark and threatening, like it has done a few times now.

"Let's go!"

As we step on the rock, I see Umberto look up again. The whites of his eyes have a bluish shine. I try to follow his gaze up to the sky. It is as if we are both trying to imagine his parents in that plane on their way to another part of the world—a part devastated by the power of the tsunami, the same ocean we were just peacefully floating in. *Can we tether them to Hawaii with our gazes?*

We are scared by the sound of an ambulance rushing through Kalakaua Avenue. We grab our towels and run back to King Kamehameha.

Day 28: Mother

"I HAVE TO tell you something," he said on the phone earlier in a distressed voice. It frustrated me that he wanted to keep it a secret.

I said, "Hey, please. Come on—just tell me."

He seems like he's on a mission to communicate to me. From the balcony, I can see him walking past the canal where we met a little over a month ago. I recognize his gait. He seems to go faster. He is a little less pulled back than usual. The sun is high in the sky, making almost no shadow underneath him. I notice he is wearing no hat.

With his face down, I can see his neck more clearly. His neck is dark, short, and wide.

It always makes me want to stretch mine up more. Dr. Shen would often emphasize the importance of stretching the upper neck vertebrae. He would say that even the Dalai Lama has a neck that is not stretched up, a sign of deviating from one's path. It needs to be stretched out and flexible. "You still need to be able to draw the three thousand characters of the Chinese alphabet with your head," Shen would say.

The screen door behind me rattles in the wind. Lennard is not home. Umberto is now straight beneath me, twelve stories down.

"Umberto!" I yell, but the sound is lost in the wind.

I catch the occasional fragrance of flowers as I look down. Across the street from King Kamehameha, squeezed right in between all those tall buildings, is a raw piece of land. A burial site, the Hawaiians say. The development of it had to stop out of respect for the *iwi*, the bones that were found. The bones contain the mana, the energy of the ancestors. Messing with them can bring repercussions to everybody involved.

***

Umberto's fist hits the bed in a reflex, defeated. His head shakes, and his eyes are fixed on the bed post. He still hasn't said a word. He rests his head on the pillow and clenches his teeth.

"What is it?" I yell. My patience is coming to an end. I want to squeeze it out of him. Whatever it is, I'm ready to push him even deeper into the pillow. He had passed me in a trance, entering the house without even looking at me. His eyes are red, more bulging then ever, as if he has cried all morning.

"She died," he mumbles.

"What? Who?"

"My mother," he whispers even softer, as if saying it louder would make it even more true, more painful, and more real.

Tears are streaming like rivers out of his eyes. He turns over and buries his head in the pillow. His big upper back starts to shake under his pale blue shirt.

"No! She died? On her trip to Atjeh? How? How?"

He lifts up his head and looks at me for the first time. His eyes are fixed, but he looks straight through me. His mouth moves hesitantly, but he is unable to produce a sound.

For a second, I dive into those eyes. It's as if he opens a door in them and lets me come inside his unbearable grief. His world is torn apart. He drops his head back against the pillow.

I feel it squeeze inside of me. *Mother? Mother?* His Hawaiian mother from the Big Island? His mother with her Ali'i background? His mother who put a protection around Umberto? His mother who we said good-bye to not even a week ago as we looked up at the airplane from the water of Waikiki? I remember how I had felt the need to tether the plane to Hawaii. I can hear it all fall now, as if the line snapped, and they got lost, a strange sense of the ground shaking under my feet.

He spoke of her with so much love, care, and tenderness. It was as if she were a fragile paper lantern and he was a child who wanted to crawl back into her lap. I gasp for air. I have to think about my mother. I feel my mother. My breath is entwined with hers. I do not know how to breathe without her. My legs start to feel weak. I feel like I am tumbling down unto the white carpet. I wonder if it is his pain or mine—or the pain of everyone who ever lost a mother. I can feel it all now.

"Mmmpffhskk." His face is still buried in the pillow.

"Come on. Talk to me. What did you say?"

"Shock. She died from shock—the devastation and seeing everything gone." He throws his arms up in the air.

Seeing everything gone echoes in my head as he runs to the bathroom.

"Umberto!" I yell as the white door closes in front of me. I hear the little golden lock turn. He cries with a deep voice, echoing in the bathroom. I am sure they must be able to hear it three stories down just like we sometimes hear their loud lovemaking in the shower, banging urgent and quickly against the wall from the newly wed Tahitian couple who sound like they are forcing a baby out of each other.

For a moment I put my ear against the door and listen to his desperate growling. I pull my head back; it is too intimate to listen to. I take a deep breath, turn my head, and look outside at the ever-waving palm trees in front of the clear blue sky. I try to imagine the aftermath of the tsunami. A world she once lived in was mercilessly eradicated. Friends, family, everything precious simply washed away, leaving a huge void that is impossible to fill. It blasted her soul into departing with all those who had already left.

I had not met her yet or the rest of his family even though they were all living on Oahu. He had shown me an old yellowed photograph of his family. He just took it out of the pocket of his jeans. A picture from West Papua, he must have been about seven years old. You could see that they were wealthy. Umberto, the eldest son, was nicely dressed with a tie around his neck. Behind him was his grim father, his sweet little mother, his brother, and his little sister. The dark faces contrasted with their white clothes. Umberto was the very darkest of them all, almost black. The white of his eyes, all white around his pupils, made him look so peculiar. It made his body float somehow.

The only thing I knew of his mother was that she was Hawaiian from the Hilo side of the Big Island, the wet side of the island. I was living on the sunny Kona side. I knew she loved to tickle his ear with a little blade of grass, something I started doing when Umberto told me about it the first week we met.

Day 33: Knocking

"DID YOU HEAR that?" Umberto looks at me. The whites of his eyes look even bigger as he points at the white door of my bedroom. We hear knocking—loud and clear, quick and urgent.

"Lennard is not at home?"

"No, there is nobody in the house. He went to Diamond Head for a showing." I hold my breath, anxious to see if there will be another knock. There is nobody in the apartment, yet we both heard a fist knocking on the wooden door.

He is still wearing his funeral clothes—a white striped shirt and silk black pants. He looks good; any man in a suit looks attractive.

Today was the ceremony for his mother. Her body was transported all the way from Indonesia back to Hawaii. Back to where she was born, back from Atjeh, back from the devastation of the tsunami. Mele Kahananui was only sixty-four years old.

"The funeral was big, family came from the Big Island, from California, and from Kauai," he said. "I could not stand to stay in my parents' house in Kailua here on the North Shore of Oahu. Everything reminds me of her. Now, she is gone … totally gone."

He looks down, beaten, and moves his feet over the fluffy carpet. His dark, flat feet have pink nails and toes that spread away from one another. The skin on his feet resembles a crackled painting. He looks down and grasps the edge of the bed for support. His shoulders slump forward. He seems to gasp for air. "I loved her so much, Christel. She was everything for me. She was always there." His tears begin to run rapidly toward the carpet. *Where were they stored in him?* His feelings so available now, as if just spilling out of a big reservoir.

"I so wish she could have met my future children," Umberto mumbles.

I swallow. An uncomfortable silence enters the room for a moment. I wonder if I heard him right. I don't want to let his words enter me. I try to make something else out of it, but I cannot.

Children? A panic races in my head. I cannot help but see an image of a little dark baby with Umberto's face on top of it, the same big eyes, same dark strong hair, same lips, and same wide nose. It makes me shiver. My throat is locked.

I don't know if I feel a squeeze in my womb from the strange knocking on the door or if it's coming from my fear of getting pregnant with him. Maybe it's the guilt toward his mother. Is wanting to be so close to her son but not wanting to mingle with his blood a betrayal against her?

I have been trying to prevent getting pregnant by Umberto almost forcefully. Each time we make love and bump flesh against flesh—with a condom, without a condom, with a torn condom, pushing him away before he came, using a diaphragm with cream, or letting him come inside of me—I know it is okay in that safe time the first five days after my period. I even used the morning-after pill one time. Every time, I send out a big conscious no to all the baby beings since I know so well that even the slightest yes, even the unconscious one, will make the conception happen.

My body wants to absorb him—everything of him—if I would let it. Being so close with him for all these weeks, making a baby together so probable. At the same time, the knowingness within me is so strong that the last thing I want is to allow anything to get in the way of the new life waiting for me on the Big Island.

I try to comfort him and put my hand on his back, not knowing what to say. My hand mechanically caresses his back through his satin shirt. I ask him why he didn't take off his funeral clothes. He shrugs. "I dunno—out of respect for her maybe."

There it is again—that knocking on the door. It is even faster now.

"That is my mother. I know it for a fact. Wait. Let me see." Umberto jumps off the bed to open the door. Nothing is there. Just the little empty hallway that seems emptier as ever.

In a flashback, I can see myself as a little girl in the bed at my aunt Angele's house, the house of my grandmother. Every night, there was a knock on her bedroom door. I was afraid of it at first, always waiting for it to come. I couldn't sleep until I had heard it. It happened at eight o'clock or later if I was not in bed.

"Oh, that is Oma." Angele would smile. Her mother, my sweet Oma, was in heaven.

"Your mother wants to show you that she is not gone at all," I say to Umberto. I am relieved that I can say something somewhat sensible, something that might ease his pain.

"Yes." A hesitant smile appears on his face as his voice trembles. "There … there she is!" Umberto's mouth falls open in slow motion, and he points at the end of the bed.

I gaze in the void, frustrated, and wonder if he is playing a trick on me. "There she is. She is waving at me."

I think about all the times I saw something that didn't seem to be there for others. I saw a little girl outside the kitchen window when I was nine years old. I yelled at my parents, convinced they would see the little girl waving behind the window, but they didn't see a thing. Just like me now.

"Oh, and now she is fading away… gone. Wow." He sighs in relief. The blanket of grief seems to disappear from his shoulders, and he jumps up on the bed like a little kid. "My mother showed herself to me, Christel!"

I see small clouds of dust coming out of the blanket in the streaming late afternoon sun.

Umberto stops, turns toward me, and looks at me in disbelief. He is still bouncing slightly up and down like a young child. When the bouncing finally stops, he says, "You really didn't see her?"

I shake my head.

Umberto jumps off the bed like Peter Pan and turns to me with his hands on his hips. "Do you smell that?"

A strong flower smell fills the room.

"Yes! Like … ginger flower, no … tuberose!" I'm happy that I can perceive it too.

"That was her favorite flower, Christel. Tuberose. The backyard was filled with it."

For a split second, I find myself in that garden filled with flowers. I'm transported in time. All three of us are together—outside time and space. In the next moment, we are back in the room.

"Strange huh?" Umberto lets himself fall on the bed again, and he embraces me tenderly. We turn toward the window as if we sense the mystery of it all in the darkening sky. So much more seems to have happened than just meeting his mother. It is as if Umberto has become reassured on a deep level and gained something instead of losing it.

"Let me take off these clothes now."

Day 35: Father

I STARE AT the pattern of the yellow tiles on the floor of the little hallway. A thousand questions run through my head. He is embracing me tight, like a monkey hugging a tree. He smells like sweat, a different kind of sweat than I know from him. He is just trying to hold on to something, anything. It feels suffocating to me. He feels so lifeless on the inside—empty and hollow, unlike the warm, soft, rich life I can sometimes taste in his usual embrace. We have grown into that embrace together.

I try to look at it intuitively. I close my eyes, but it is hard to stay neutral. It all becomes a blur. Did the Papuan artifacts in his father's house come alive and beg him to follow? Was the tsunami from six weeks ago echoing in everything? Had losing his loving Hawaiian wife along with the other twenty-one family members become too much for Umberto's father? It all becomes a blur. I imagine his lifeless body on the wooden floor this morning at six. It was a heart attack, and his neighbor found him.

Was his wife asking him to join her? Were all those family members calling him to be loyal and follow in the aftermath of the tsunami?

"I hate him, and now he died." Umberto grunts and runs away.

I let the door close behind me and run after him with no key in my pocket. "Umberto!" I yell. "Let me come with you!"

He lifts his hand to hail a cab at the end of Kalani and steps in.

I reach the cab in time to tap the dark window before it leaves. The last thing I see are his big eyes, helpless, looking at me as the cab pulls away.

Day 42: Phone

"I BOUGHT A new phone today." Umberto waves with the little thing in his hand.

If we are not at my place, we always meet somewhere in between. I don't like his place. I have been there only once. I can feel it creeping up on me. He lives with four other Indonesians in a dark and messy house that smells like meat and rice. They have dark sheets for curtains across the windows, letting no daylight in.

We are walking from his house to mine; the evening is warm, and the street is poorly lit.

"You can make pictures with it, but I have no clue how it works. Do you know?" He gives the little Samsung phone to me. I have no clue either, but I take the phone and look at the screen.

"It is usually very simple with those things. You go to Menu, then to Pictures, and then …" I click from one thing to another and take a random picture. "Yay! It worked!" I bring the little screen closer to my face. "Huh? What is that?" I concentrate on the little screen. I look around us. There is nobody in the street, just an uneven sidewalk bordering a dark empty piece of land to the right of us where a streetlight is not working. I look at the screen again. I can clearly see a little girl, all in white, with an old-fashioned lace dress. She must be about five years old. I hold my breath. It is very clear against the dark black night around her. Together we look at the little girl.

"Just an angel!" I exclaim. I look at the spot where I took the picture—not a single trace.

Umberto squints at the screen.

I put my arm around his shoulder and my face against his. I feel so excited. "Do you see what I see? We just took a picture of a little angel!" I call out loud, almost wanting others to hear me. I look up at the building next to the open piece of land. A few lights are on, but nobody is outside at this hour.

Umberto grabs the phone, squeezes it, and pushes all the little buttons. "This cannot be. I need to erase it!"

"What do you mean?" I laugh. "It clearly appears on the little screen. There is nothing to deny. Let me look at it again."

"No!" He pushes me away, his eyes red and spitting fire.

I step back.

"Leave it! It is my phone."

"Come on, Umberto. Why are you upset?"

We stand across from each other—a deep black gap of misunderstanding opening between us, making the dark night even more black.

"It is such a beautiful thing! I think she must have a message for us if she is showing herself, and you act like it is evil!" I reach out my arms to hold him, but he turns his back, grunting as he walks away.

"Gone."

It is too late. Gone. The picture is gone—deleted from the phone—as if it never existed. He puts the phone back in his pocket.

"Wait. Maybe ..." It is still in the trash; I wanted to say. But the wall between us has become too big.

"Let's walk on," Umberto mumbles. "I don't want to talk about it."

In silence, we continue to my house. "What is it that you don't wanna talk about? You seem to know so much more."

When we enter Kalani Avenue, he stops. "I am gonna go home." He gives me a quick kiss on the mouth.

"Wait a minute. It is one thing that you don't want to talk about it, but now you want to go home? You want to let this beautiful, precious thing ruin our night?" My irritation shows as I get louder.

I watch his dark blue shirt with the yellow letters HFD, the Honolulu Fire Department, disappear into the dark night. I realize there is no way of holding him back. Something has got to him, and whatever it is goes really deep. This cannot be. The words and his panic repeat in my mind. Something burst forth from a place he would rather have kept closed off, presenting itself from beyond. It needs to be kept there—no matter what.

It's a leak in a great dam of mystery. And this leak needs to be fixed. He doesn't want it for himself, and he doesn't want me to see it.

It is not just a picture of a little angel. How could it have sparked his fear so deeply? What could send him shuffling away into the night, screwing up our date? A little being presented herself from elsewhere in our world so clearly. Is he possessed? Is something else trying to have a grip? For Umberto, the unseen world is such a reality, just like it is for me.

I wonder what her message is.

Day 49: New Life

FINALLY, I RETURN to the Big Island. It is the youngest and biggest of the seven Hawaiian Islands, the one with the active volcano, the one with the most profound and primal energy. It has deserts, snow, and rain forests. It has a dry side and a wet side—and twelve different climates. The island is full of growth and possibility. Every day, new black land is created. I want my new life to start on the island that called to my soul and invited me to come in the first place.

I can pick up where I left off, after the distractions of Ravindu, the magician, after having to go back to Holland to renew my visa, after marrying Lennard, after meeting Umberto, and after the strange relationship in Waikiki that followed. I can leave it all behind now.

I put my feet in the little pool and balance on the black lava stone with my hands on my hips. How different it feels to stand here right now, how much more free. The yoke of my concerns about permanent residency is lifted from my shoulders. The question is no longer if I am really able to stay here, or how am I going to do it? I am back on the Big Island, and the world is at my feet. The ocean is at my feet. Lennard will be living with me here off and on.

I felt so excited returning to the Big Island this morning. The ocean looked so appealing that I decided to drive down to the City of Refuge. My favorite spot is a little coral beach. The black lava makes a perfect basin, protected from the ocean. Almost seamlessly, the blue mass of water transforms into land. There is scarcely any difference in height; the flat black stones are only a subtle elevation from the water.

I always feel like the ocean is higher than me—as if I am sitting beneath it. It is like looking into an aquarium. It is wonderful to be at the same height as the water. My eyes are just above the surface, looking over the immense body of water in front of me. It is mysteriously lit by the hazy afternoon sun. The horizon is not visible like most days on the Big Island. It is blurred by the emissions from the volcano, which is called the *vog*.

There is nobody to be seen, and the water is so calm. I let myself float on my back in the little basin and close my eyes. In my mind, I feel Waikiki washing out of me like long threads, bubbles, and little pieces. I was there almost two months before Lennard dropped me off at the airport. He will come here in a month. Having him bring me to "the other side" felt so symbolic. Now I am a permanent resident, and all the insecurities about my status are gone. I look at the water drops sliding off my tanned body. This body can stay here forever. It feels so new and beautifully tanned and shiny. It is as if I can feel myself more than ever. I am more beautiful than I ever was. Slowly, I emerge from the water in my new state. Finally, I am back on the island where I so wanted to be. I was pulled all the way from Holland by the whisper that called me here, where the old, blind kahuna told me I have a unique thing to do. I nestle on my towel on the big pieces of coral.

In a reflex, I take my pen and notebook out of my bag. I sigh. My relationship with Umberto is over forever now too. The strange relationship started two months ago with our peculiar meeting the day before I got married. Like a movie flashback, fragments play in my mind. Everything is surrounded by a cloud of confusion and doubt.

My pen glides over the paper. At the moment when I want to put a final line under everything with Umberto, it comes out of me: the whisper. It feels like it is dictating to me: *"You have known each other for a long time, have been brought together again, and will rapidly enter a series of experiences. It will reach far beyond your current comprehension, and it will expand your consciousness in many ways. You will be a witness. He will be a servant. In the end, you will not be together. Umberto knows this. You have access to the database of self-determination. Every time it will be about vibration and choice. The choice that he makes will be very different to yours."*

Then it stopped. Nothing comes out of my pen anymore. It is as if the ink is finished. The voice has disappeared, perhaps diving under the water in front of me. Black handwritten letters have flowed from my fountain pen onto the white page. I wanted to dedicate that page to a whole new chapter in my life: my new status, my new future, my island that I finally returned to. I just wanted to dedicate one sentence to the door that I just closed—the short chapter with Umberto in Waikiki—and now I have polluted the virgin white paper with these words.

I want to call after it. "Yes, but I don't want it. I just want to put an end to it. It is finished. I want to be finished with all these vague feeling between us." Indignantly, I read what I wrote. What just appeared on the paper. It certainly doesn't feel like I wrote it myself. *Entering a few experiences? What could that mean?*

I live on an entirely different island, hundreds of miles away. I cannot see myself going back to Honolulu, and he will never come here because of the curse. Such a meeting would be very unlikely.

The only thing that remains in my head is his eyes. I so loved those eyes. They often reminded me of the drawing classes at art school. The art classes in which I always wanted to go beyond the paper—the white paper that was never big enough. I wanted to show that which existed beyond the boundaries of the paper. Now I recognize it in these eyes: eyes that seem to float endlessly, undefined, eyes without boundaries.

This morning, Umberto and I said good-bye for the last time. I can still see us sitting there on one of the many benches of Waikiki. Our relationship seemed to largely consist of meetings on little benches: the first meeting on that bench along the Ala Wai Canal, the benches in the park, along the water, in Diamond Head, in the Chinese restaurant, at the airport. Our final bench was at Sans Souci Beach this morning. I wanted to visit my favorite beach one more time. In French, it is the "without worries" beach. That is where we said good-bye.

"I am going to leave in an hour, Lennard will take me to the airport," I said.

He responded by shrugging.

That reaction was enough for me. His indifferent gaze at the armrest of the bench, one of the only benches with an armrest, made me so angry inside. His leg unconsciously shot forward as if he wanted to kick something out of the way. Why didn't he beg me on his knees to stay? Why didn't he take my hand?

At the same time, his gesture was perfect. It became so easy for me to say farewell to him today. We embraced for a little while and then walked away in opposite directions: me toward the ocean and him toward the mountains.

Forty-Nine Days

FOR SEVEN STEADY years before my move to Hawaii, I had my own acupuncture practice in the center of Maastricht, in the very south of Holland. I wasn't really treating people just for the headache, infertility, back pain, or sleeplessness they came through the door with. I didn't see them as bodies in need of fixing. For me, their pain was an expression of a voice that wanted to be heard. I could see that voice by reading their tongues and hear even more by feeling the tightness, rhythm, fullness, hollowness, and depth of their pulses. I loved to put my ring, middle, and index fingers on their pulses to hush their talking and let their bodies speak. I could hear their livers grumble, the stomachs cry out, and their bladders push to create a territory.

During my seven years as an acupuncturist, I had a fascination with chronopuncture, the rhythm of change that runs through the body or "needling at the right time." To facilitate this, I had people come at the strangest times. I'd needle the most favorably indicated point in just the right place and at just the right time when they came to get a shoulder, a headache, or infertility fixed. Just like the perfect cogwheels of a clock meshing together, that's how I felt when doing chronopuncture. It was like two wheels meeting at one little point in time.

I see meeting Umberto as wheels that meet in one moment in time. We were two cogs on two enormous wheels coming together in one moment in time.

To be exact, we only spent forty-nine days together, over a period of two months, from the moment we met till the moment I left the island. Seven times seven days. We spent Forty-nine days together in our bodies on Oahu, the most crowded place in Hawaii, which is known as "the gathering place," in Honolulu, or more precise in Waikiki: a little tiny strip of land.

It is as if a magnifying glass was suspended over my life for me to look through. Every detail is a world; every detail colorfully dazzles with intense focus. It is magnified by the way the light is in Honolulu. It seems like everything shines. Lennard's convertible car, sunglasses, men, women, the palm trees, the ocean so different from the way the light is on the Big Island. So different from the light in Holland, where the skies are always cloudy like Rembrandt's paintings.

I had never perceived coincidences so clearly. It had nothing to do with being madly in love. For the first time in my life, I—who could so easily fall in love with every man in my path—arrived at a state of being that I would call "a reserved curiousness." After my love-lust interlude with Ravindu, the magician who stole me away to Vegas, I was cured from surrendering to a man and getting distracted from my goals.

But I was tremendously intrigued by the two worlds represented in Umberto—Papuan, with its Dutch-Indonesian history and Hawaiian. He was connected to where I came from and where I was going. Despite that, I did not think we were a good match.

Forty-nine days, and then the wheel turned…

Part 2

The Chat

OLYMPIC SPORTSMEN, COACHES, police officers, schoolteachers, businessmen, and artists have been passing through my Qigong retreats on the Big Island. Now there are two psychologists: tall, dark Sandra and short, blonde Jennie.

"This is someone else, and they are playing a game with you!" Jennie says in a tone that reminds me of my junior schoolteacher. She gestures toward the mysterious writing on my laptop.

"Yes, it's a joke," Sandra adds, but her eyes tell a different truth.

"What? A joke? A joke about … *this*?" as I swallow the word "death."

"Do not do it. You cannot talk to the dead," Jennie says sternly, taking the words directly off the screen of my mind. The reality of what is happening has penetrated her, and she nervously lights a cigarette. She exhales a huge cloud of gray smoke, which is carried directly into my face by the wind.

"Sorry! Phhhhhhhhhhhhhhhhh … I don't believe it, I think it's scary."

"What do you mean you don't believe it? How does he know that I am crying?"

I had learned to trust that voice. The whisper was always there at crucial moments. If I had to locate it, I would place it near to the top of my head. Sometimes it speaks to me from just above my head. Sometimes it is very clear, at other times, it is faint. There is something unshakeable in it. It is strong with seniority and the wisdom of the ages. When I am ready to cross a border or head into the unknown, it always says, "Just trust me."

And it is there again. It is loud and clear, and I know I can trust it. I know this is happening. This is true. Umberto is talking to me from heaven. I can talk back on the computer. The letters appear rapidly on my screen—as if written with a feather in real time, word by word, letter by letter, one inch tall, in white. The rest of the screen seems to vibrate—as if getting ready to disappear. There is no frame besides the little frame underneath his brother's conversation: "Umberto appears to be offline."

"It is me Umberto. Why are you crying?"

His handwritten words appear again on the screen. "Why are you crying?" They fill the whole screen from left to right. It looks like his beautiful handwriting. I glare at the keyboard to see if the keys are being pushed. No. I take a deep breath and try to push my tears away.

Umberto sees that I am crying. His body is dead—hundreds of miles away from me. He sees me. He can see that I am crying on the Big Island.

"I think you are too young to die. That is why I cry." My fingers tremble as I type the letters in the Yahoo messenger box. I feel as if I am touching his compact body. I realize the absurdity of this statement. Who am I to say that? *Too young to die?* What has age to do with it anyway? I smile wryly.

A warm gush is flowing through my body. It is as if he is there with me. Over my back and down in my belly—the love for everything as I knew him for that short period of time. His dark skin is next to mine. Our connection is oozing through these strange, magical letters on my old computer screen. All of our encounters were filled with magic—despite the differences of my lightness next to his depression.

"They are calling me. My family is calling me."

I stare at the black screen, trying to imagine, as I repeat what just appeared in front of me. *Calling?*

"All these people are calling me, Christel. There is such a beautiful music. I am dancing. I am so happy. But why are you crying?"

All these people? Like all the ones who lost their lives in the tsunami? I can almost feel it. It is like a wave—an energetic tsunami pulling souls to the other side. And now it is his turn! Wave after wave after wave. Three weeks after the tsunami, his mother. Three weeks later, his father. And now Umberto ... another three weeks, another wave.

I bend forward and shout at my laptop in Dutch. My mouth almost touches the screen. "Okay, Umberto. It may be that you are dancing with angels there in heaven, but I think you don't have to go yet. It is too early. You still have a choice. A choice to be alive." I want to enter the world where he is right now. For a moment, I grab the screen and move it back and forth to see if his world really appears behind it. Then I slump, dropping my body back as I realize how silly it is.

"I love you so much, my lilikoi." My lilikoi. I feel a chill down my spine.

I feel so embraced by him. *I love you.* I can almost hear the way he pronounced it with a little Hawaiian accent, the warm timbre, almost mumbling. We never went there before. We never said it to each other. Always dancing around those words, both of us were afraid of the consequence: to get too attached or make it all too real. He would just say "My lilikoi." Lilikoi is the Hawaiian word for passion fruit.

"You can choose, Umberto! You can make a choice. You can make a statement that you want to be alive," I type.

"But I am happy here where I am."

"Why did I come into your life?"

Surprised I look at the last sentence I typed. What a strange question. At the same time, it was so appropriate, I had to ask it. And now that I see it appear on my screen, it is as if somehow we both touched upon a whole different level of our accidental meeting the day before I got married.

The conversation stopped. I look at the time: 9.30. *Half an hour! Half an hour after we first started talking, but it only felt like five minutes.* His last letters right in the middle of my screen were big and alive, almost breathing.

"I love you."

I imagine Umberto dancing between angels, his chubby face moving around, and his body like a puppet underneath it. He is dancing on a cloud.

Anxiously I keep looking at the screen, hoping to enter this "other world" through the glass surface, but nothing happens. The last letters I typed keep on echoing in my mind. *Why did I come into your life?* The image of that strange message flowing out of my pen a few days ago appears again in my mind's eye, telling me it is not over between us. What did it say again? Something about going through experiences … expanding consciousness … being a witness … something about choice. Fragments like a trace of the message again, but I intuitively grab my phone and cross the street to the only place where my cell phone has reception. With every step, another question pops into my mind. How could it be? How could Umberto be talking to me on the computer? Where did he die? How did he end up in the hospital? How did his family get to him so quickly? How come he had a heart attack?

I sit on a little lava rock bench in the empty lot between the vines. Strange. I have all these questions about the reality of his body, but it seems not to matter at all. He was chatting with me from heaven. He is still the boy who experiences life as something that just happens to him, wondering: "How did I end up here?" He is following his ancestors in that deadly wave.

And I was just typing to heaven. And then there was the fear that my two retreat ladies showed. The disbelief. And the whisper told me so clearly: "Just talk back to him." That moment I knew for sure: this is true.

As I take a deep breath, my phone rings and I am astounded to see Umberto's number. Another deep breath ... imagine, imagine that ... no ... that cannot be true. My voice trembles when I pick up the phone.

"Hello?"

His voice was faint. "It is me, Umberto. I am back! We have been talking to each other, right?"

"Umberto?"

What does he mean, *talking? Typing* he means. *After five minutes, your brain will be permanently damaged, scientists say. Has he become crazy?* No, he doesn't sound like it. He is absolutely himself. He just sounds weak and soft.

I push my little phone against my ear. I'm irritated by the noise of the waves in front of me, and the lava rocks seem too hard. I look behind me. Sandra and Jennie are nowhere to be seen. The lights in the house are off. They must have scuttled off to bed.

"I could hear your voice."

"What did you say?" I yell.

"I am back in my body."

"You are back? You were dead—and now you are alive again? Where are you?"

"I am in the hospital. I could hear your voice. It is so beautiful there."

"Hear my voice?" I try to scream above the waves.

Voice? My voice! He can remember everything I typed, and he heard it as my voice—even though I only used my voice when I said I wasn't agreeing with that energetic tsunami in Dutch.

Before I can say anything else, he says, "I saw you taking a shower at seven thirty."

Permission?

I LOOK AROUND me in the small plane. Next to me, a beautifully muscled Hawaiian tells me that he is on his way to an ultimate fighting game. He smiles proudly at me and uncovers his perfect white teeth, showing that he is determined to be victorious. I smile and nod back at him.

"And what are you going to do in Honolulu?" he asks.

"Well, I am going to meet a friend." I quickly finish my sentence, surprised by my reaction. My voice is muffled. I have a strange squeezing in my belly and a big lump in my throat. I try to swallow. This guy is not waiting to hear about a dead boyfriend. My teeth clench involuntary, my breath becomes superficial, and I want to push myself back against the chair. My eyes rest at his tapping fingers on his strong knees. He rubs his legs, measuring and activating his strength.

In one moment, the disapproval on the faces of Sandra and Jennie flashes by. Despite this man's openness, I absolutely cannot tell him the true reason for my visit. In my mind, I say, "Oh, I am just going to visit my friend who just made the choice to not join this energetic tsunami, and that is why after two hours being dead he decided to come back from heaven, after communicating about it through chatting on the computer." Ha! Chatting on the computer? No one would believe me!

I chuckle and stretch in my chair. The friendly guy lifts his eyebrows and looks at me. The conversation stops abruptly. He looks out the window and smiles again, apparently thrilled about his upcoming fight. I see his teeth glistening and his determination not to get distracted.

I glance over the people in the plane. Who, out of all these people, would understand my experience? I scan the plane, look at it intuitively, and try to get in touch with the overall consensus reality. I feel the pressure like we sometimes do in a reading at the Sixth Sense Center: the pressure of no permission, of denial, a mental barrier that is almost palpable in the air. I look at a strongly built white tourist in a Hawaiian shirt. His hat is pulled over his face. He is asleep with a closed book on his lap. I try to bend over and read the title, but I cannot see it. His corpulent wife is wearing the same shirt and looks out the window, her face sweaty and a little worried. How would it be if I told her?

"My boyfriend died and came back from heaven after chatting with me on the computer."

"Oh, really? How was it?"

"It was great. He just decided not to follow his ancestors in that deadly tsunami."

The woman turns her head abruptly; a greasy curl falls down in her face, and sweat drips from her forehead. As if sensing my energy, she squeezes her eyes for a moment, pulling up a wall between us. Here we are, flying through the sky—something that was once unimaginable—, yet here we are, defying laws of gravity.

My ears start to pop from the descent. I hear a high tone, and then all the noise is numbed out. I am floating in a void. The Hawaiian guy looks at me and points at his ears.

I nod. "I know. I am deaf too."

In this isolation, it starts to dawn to me that this group of people actually represents "the world." When I'm back on solid ground again, it will not be any different. I sigh. Who will believe me? Will they say that I am crazy? They will say that somebody is playing a trick on me. It is medically proven that a body cannot be without oxygen for more than a few minutes. The brain stem will be permanently damaged. A body cannot think without a brain. They will say that I am being manipulated.

"We are ready for landing," a friendly voice says over the intercom.

For a moment, I am overwhelmed by emotions. My ears pop open again. In a few more moments, I will really see him: the embodiment of a miracle. My heart is pounding in my throat, and I feel extremely quiet. I can still say yes to this big wall of denial. It is as if it is still calling me. You still can go back. You can walk away from it. You can pretend nothing ever happened. It is clear; deep inside, I made the choice a long time ago. I take a deep breath and walk toward the arrival hall with my neck stretched up.

I haven't even talked with his family about it yet. I haven't met or spoken to them at all. I was just too absorbed by the rest of the retreat and the two women in the past nine days. I only talked twice with Jennie and Sandra about Umberto after it happened. It was too sensitive a subject, and it took them a lot of time to digest. At first, they were still in denial about it. During the last day, it seemed like their boundaries had fallen away by just being in Hawaii. They somehow accepted the idea of the incredible communication.

The whole week, I felt a strong urge to see Umberto—not really to be with him, fall in love, or return to my life in Waikiki, but I just want to see him with my own eyes. Only then would it be real. I wanted to find proof somehow. Did this really happen? Did he change? I booked the ticket to go see him the minute the retreat was over. I needed to look him in the eyes, see it for myself, and even smell heaven on him. They say newborn babies smell like where they came from. I will return to my life on the Big Island the very next day.

There he is. Umberto is back in his body and sitting on a little bench: no fanfare, bells, choirs of angels, or flower leis. No cheering crowd. He is just sitting on the bench in his black jeans and a white shirt. The first thing that strikes me is that he looks so alone. The crowd of tourists seems to disappear around him. There is something else. It seems like he is emanating light! Is it my imagination?

I come closer, give him a big hug, and realize that nothing has changed. The closer I come, the more ordinary he is. He still feels exactly the same. He's still the guy I said good-bye to for good only two weeks ago. We haven't said a word yet—not even hello. As if the silence he experienced orchestrated this moment for us, we just hold each other for a long time. Is there something different? Is there light and softness around him that I never noticed before? Did his dark skin seem a little pale?

His strong shoulder pushes against me on the bus to Waikiki. He doesn't say a word on the way to our favorite Chinese restaurant. We are holding hands and smiling at each other. Every word seems superfluous. I cannot keep my eyes off of his hand. His hand is a little drier than usual. A whitish hue covers the chocolate color. *This is a hand that was dead!*

A big teapot and two little cups are put in front of us. Umberto starts, as somebody coming back from a long voyage oversees. He seems to remember everything of our conversation.

"And then you said to me—"

"No," I say, smiling. "Then I typed you back."

"Huh? What typing? What do you mean?"

"Well, just like I said. I received a message from you with handwritten letters all across my computer screen, and I was typing you back. Just like we sometimes did with Yahoo Messenger. Just a normal chat."

He looks at me with big eyes. "So you didn't really talk to me then?"

"No, just in my thoughts and on the computer."

"Wow. I could literally hear everything! I could hear your voice very clearly!"

We look at each other and burst out laughing. His white teeth are all exposed, and I almost roll off my chair. A few people in the restaurant look at our table and continue with their conversations. Being with Umberto always seems like from another reality: tangible but hard to grasp.

"I have to tell you something." Umberto looks down at his cup of tea. "Remember when we took that picture of that little girl?"

"Yes, that was about a month ago—and you didn't know how fast to erase it!"

"Exactly! That girl on the picture was there! She was waiting for me on the other side. I recognized her immediately, with her hair so full and beautiful. Her name is Karen. She told me that she is there to help me as a guide. She has been with me since birth. And she told me about her last life. She could tell me exactly where she died when she was seven. Her parents were so sad. She decided immediately to be a guide for me!"

I blink and let his words sink in for a moment. "Wow. She announced herself three weeks before your death! She wanted to show herself but not leave any trace. And that is the reason why you were so desperately trying to erase the picture. Why do you think she wanted to be your guide?"

"Because of her parents' grief, she wasn't able to leave earth completely. It was almost that they didn't allow her. She had a choice to become a guide or incarnate again. She chose to become a guide for me because we have the same pattern. I don't know what it means. I still feel her very close to me. It gave me a very comforting feeling when I was on the other side."

89

Umberto pours another cup of green tea. He seems to be so much more confident and much more familiar with the ground I am familiar with.

"This is fantastic. Do you see there was a meaning behind it?" I am sitting on the edge of my chair, and I feel a hundred questions arise in me. *How was it? Who did you meet? What did the doctors say?* I want to know everything. The questions just seem to disappear while we're together. We are together as if we are still lovers, as if nothing ever happened, as if I never moved to another island. For a moment, an uncomfortable confusion arises in me. We were not together anymore. I made such a clear decision. *What is left of that?* Frustrated, my mind is looking for a way to analyze the reason for us being together right now. At the same time, there is utter euphoria. I sigh deeply, and it starts to dawn on me that there is a much deeper meaning behind this strange relationship that surpasses every logical explanation. I take my last sip of tea.

"Let's get some food."

"Oh, you cannot even imagine how hungry I was when I came back. It was as if my body hadn't eaten for days. Everything needed to catch up, and I was only gone for two hours."

An older couple looks up at us, catching a few of Umberto's words. I wonder what they are thinking. Two people are just leaving from the lazy sofas that are also part of the dining area.

I laugh when I let myself fall onto the comfortable sofa.

"Why are you laughing?" Umberto asks.

"If they only knew what you were talking about!"

Umberto is trying to smile, but it seems like he doesn't get it, which makes me laugh even more.

The friendly waiter has a nice aura around him as he hands us the menu. I move a little closer to Umberto, put my arm around his shoulder, and push my face against his. We look at the pictures on the menu; every dish is presented as a beautiful little picture, a perfect piece of art.

My thoughts start to wander, and I try to imagine what Umberto's eyes have seen. I want to crawl in them and see what he has seen. My body starts to tremble. For a split second, I feel myself merge with his experience. It is still so fresh in him. Can I look with him into heaven—or was it just the idea that made me tremble?

There are a million questions in my head, but none of them seem relevant. All those questions result in the frustration of not being able to get to the core of what actually had happened. I bend over and kiss him softly on the lips.

***

I had booked a cheap hotel right next to the Chinese restaurant, for one night. We enter the elevator without speaking a word. After that kiss in the restaurant there is actually nothing profound we can talk about. We just want to celebrate being back together. Again we start to kiss passionately, our tongues playing with each other. He is holding me tight. *Blood? What is that? I actually can taste blood in my mouth.* How is that possible? But before I can say something Huberth steps back.

"Aw!" He pushes me away and grasps his chest. I feel frightened.

The elevator doors open and close again without us getting out. He looks at me as if he wants to hide something. I can see the pain on his face.

"What is the matter?" I yell. I push the button again to open the doors. We are at the fifth floor. Holding his chest, he gestures for me to open room 503. It is a simple, tasteless room with cheap Hawaiian prints everywhere. He jumps on the bed and leans back against the wall.

"I have to tell you something." He catches his breath and sighs. "I have lung cancer, and I have to be operated on." He falls back on the bed and watches the ceiling fan.

I am speechless. The blood seems to flow backward in my body, and everything freezes. I cannot help but taste the blood in my mouth. *Cancer? Yikes.* I taste it again. It is proof of Umberto's cancer. I squeeze my lips together. *I just tasted blood. His cancer. Am I contaminated now?* I want to run to the toilet and vomit. I hold my breath in horror and wonder how long I can do that. I don't want it. I don't want to breathe it. I don't want to swallow it. I don't want to feel his blood with cancer. I don't care that cancer is maybe not in his blood. I don't want to taste this. I feel guilty.

"What?" My mind is racing, and I try to analyze the blood in my mouth again. "What? You just came back from death, and you got a new life. Everything is okay right now, right? You are the embodiment of a miracle!"

He says, "When I was brought into the hospital, they did a scan and found cancer on my lung. It is a dangerous small cell cancer, and it is already fully developed. It has to be removed as soon as possible." All the

91

euphoria of being unconquerable is gone. The room now looks even more tasteless and foreign.

"It is my right lung." Umberto looks down at the floor.

"Right lung," I whisper, still not wanting to swallow the blood. I am starting to feel dizzy. It strikes me that the strange black cloud always seemed visible on the right side. Would it be related? I wonder. It had happened a few times now: a black shadow next to his head, like a swarm of flies, a bat, or a dark cloud. It gave me chills. When I concentrated on it, it was gone. Everything on an energetic level is perceived better from the corner of our eyes.

He will have the tests this week and the operation next week. His breath is a little shorter than before, but he blames it on not surfing so much anymore. He just has a little pain in his chest now and then, but he never would have guessed that it could be cancer. The doctors blame it on dangerous vapors, paint, and asbestos from when he used to be a painter in Indonesia.

I know that it is just a little part of the truth. There is so much more to it than just asbestos poisoning. That black cloud has everything to do with it. I know it for sure!

"Shall we still open the bottle of wine that you brought?" I whisper. "At least you have conquered death. Why not conquer this one too? You did make the choice to come back to life. Now you can choose to become totally healthy again, right?"

A faint smile appears on Umberto's face and he stands up to open the bottle. I look at his slightly bent posture. *Cancer.* My mind is occupied by this word. The taste of blood lingers in my mouth. The good feeling we had this afternoon has vanished. Umberto is not a miracle anymore; the idea that he can conquer anything has dissipated. Umberto is really sick and will need an operation just like everybody else with lung cancer. Now that I am so close to him and even taste his blood in my mouth—in our sweet kiss—the illness reveals itself in me. It is a totally different story. Gone is the idea that miracles are possible.

"I will use the glasses from the bathroom." He looks delighted when he comes back with the two plastic glasses.

"Cheers! To life!" With our arms around each other, we both take a sip. I try to rinse the residue of blood from my mouth. I hope that the wine disinfects my whole body.

Taxi

"TO THE AIRPORT," I say to the taxi driver. We sit in the back, his compact hand in mine. Umberto leans back and looks at the roof of the car.

"I will really come and visit you there on the Big Island," he mumbles.

"Okay, but then you need to bring your delightful body with you!"

"What do you mean?"

"Well, exactly what I say. When only your spirit visits, it's not so good. Like you see me in the shower, and I cannot even see you!"

"I was actually embracing you tightly."

"For real?" I look straight at Umberto.

"Yes, why?" He turns his head back to the yellow roof again.

"When I was in the shower and you saw me, right after you died, I was actually thinking about our relationship. It was totally over. I really had decided that I didn't want to see you anymore after I left Honolulu. When I was standing there in the shower, all these vivid memories came back—all the wonderful lovemaking for hours in the shower. You always knew to touch me in exactly the right spot. My body so wanted to melt with yours. And now, it appears we had exactly the same thought at that moment! Although you were apparently dead." I chuckle. "It was not so much just my thought. It was *our* thought together! It was actually a whole vivid experience! Wow. You were really there. That is why it felt so intimate!"

"Yeah. It couldn't be more real. I was there with everything that I am!"

"Well, except your body!"

"Hawaiian Airlines!" the taxi driver says.

I stare at Umberto. The taxi driver overheard our whole conversation.

"That's twelve dollars." He turns around and looks at us from tip to toe with his curious face. He must be Vietnamese with these fine lines on his face. Hastily I hand him the money and leave the car. Umberto puts my suitcase in front of me. The man gets back into the car, but he doesn't leave. Clearly he can sense something and he seems startled by what we were just talking about. I lean forward again and start to give him a friendly wave. As if he feels caught, he pushes the gas pedal and rushes off.

"He didn't know what he was hearing." I laugh.

Dogs

I AM BACK in my new life on the Big Island. On my short visit to Honolulu, I went to the apartment to spend some time with Lennard. He waved enthusiastically at me with a letter in his hand. "Yoo-hoo. Your work permit is here!"

It felt like another door had opened, and although I was surviving well enough by giving retreats, I decided on my flight back to the Big Island that I wanted a job. The choice was easy. When I saw the stewardess delivering water and juice, I got it: I wanted to be a waitress. I always wanted to experience it, and I knew the perfect place. The Aloha Angel Café was in a big pink building in the little town Kainaliu, right up the hill from where I live. It has a cinema and a café for breakfast and dinner. The waitresses have wings drawn on their colorful T-shirts. I always liked the atmosphere, buzzing with aliveness. The outside lanai has a great view of the ocean, and the guests are welcomed by little green geckos walking over the tables and begging for jam or honey.

On Monday morning, I sat at the little desk across from the boss. On Tuesday morning, I put on my black apron and red shirt with wings on the back, ready for my new adventure. I love everything about my new job: the fast pace, learning how to juggle plates, getting to know my colleagues, seeing the friendly faces of guests each morning, and getting a check each week. Above all, I enjoy the fact that I am establishing myself on the Big Island in my new life.

I quickly develop a nice routine. I swim with the dolphins early in the morning in front of the blue house that I am housesitting. I go to work and take night classes at the Sixth Sense Center in South Point.

Honolulu and Umberto have almost disappeared from my mind. After my third day of work and a refreshing dive in the ocean, I open my e-mail. To my surprise, I see an e-mail from Umberto's aunt: "Emergency," He has only told me about her a few times.

Dear Christel,

> *I know Umberto and you are good friends, so I want to let you know what happened to him this morning. As you know, he had a lung operation today. It did not go well, and he entered a coma. He is in the Honolulu hospital. I will keep you informed if anything changes. Let's pray for him.*

Moana Kahananui.

In a trance, I read the message. I feel my heart sink. A coma? I read it a few times. The word *coma* almost jumps off the page. Without hesitation, I decide to call the hospital. I take my phone to the only spot where there is cell reception, which is right next to the ocean.

"Umberto Sihirbaz? Yes, he is here, we have no information about him right now," the woman from the hospital with a typical Hawaiian accent sounds so unreal and detached. It is as if it is not a case of life and death. It is like she is talking about my bank statement, and I somehow like it.

When I hang up, I feel strange. The urge to fly to Honolulu is gone. I have a job now. I am not able to leave so easily. Do I really want to see him again? Do I really want to confront the reality of his body? Do I want to see him on machines in a coma? Do I still want to be with him at all? We said good-bye again a week ago—good-bye forever. I wished him good luck with his operation, and that was it.

Lost in thought, I walk back to the house, back to my laptop. The message from Aunty Moana is still open in my mailbox. And that is when what I already expected happens, almost immediately. Now there is no witness, no Sandra or Jennie to see me, I am alone.

On the screen I see: "I smell plumeria. You smell like plumeria. Are you there, Christel?"

How does he know I am at my laptop? Right here upstairs in my bedroom? Again my whole screen turns black, and handwritten letters appear, again only the little Yahoo box down below is visible. I hold my breath and put my hand on my chest. I am still wearing my bikini from my earlier swim, and I notice little grains of sand on my skin. My mouth falls open. In awe, I see the somewhat familiar letters appear again on my screen. Instantly, the rest of the doubt about needing to go see him falls away. *This is him, and he is here talking to me.*

What? Umberto recognizes me as plumeria? I take another breath and hold it again. One of my most favorite scents in Hawaii is the beautiful plumeria. His body is on machines in the Honolulu hospital, and I am here hundreds of miles away on the Big Island. He is floating in between realities, balancing between life and death in a coma. And my scent called him like deceased grandfathers who make themselves known by a cigar smell or grandmothers with eau de cologne.

With a mix of strange nervousness and excitement, my stiff fingers type back in the little Yahoo frame: "Yes, I am here. Where are you?"

"Oh, now I can hear your voice."

"It works," I yell. "It works again!"

"I am here in this place called the garden. I am just sitting here. It is so peaceful. I know this place so well somehow, and I know I can talk to you from here. Can you hear me? It is as if all the flowers and plants I love are here: plumeria, gardenia, bamboo, hibiscus. Oh, and there are my dogs."

The words come as fast and as clear as it can be: "My body is in the hospital on machines. The lung operation hadn't gone well, but I am here in this place I call the garden." The letters appear at a high pace on my screen.

The absurdity of it all—the impossibility, the unexplainable—somehow finds a place in me. I feel split in two. On the one hand, there is a strange calmness in me. Do I just need to step into it and be a witness? In the back of my mind, a merry-go-round spins and spins at a higher and higher pace, spitting out this blur. It goes around and around, faster and faster. I wish my friends in Holland could see me like this. I am talking to heaven—or almost heaven—to a guy in a coma. I am chatting to heaven, and Umberto can talk back! I feel more connected to Umberto than ever. Wow! If this is possible with technology, what if this becomes the new … I cannot wait to tell everyone at the Sixth Sense Center!

I am doing what I was talking about fifteen years ago when I wrote my final paper at the School of Arts in Maastricht about virtual reality: In "The Disappearing Body," I pondered the possibility of being able to communicate with a spirit without a body through a computer. It was before the Internet, cell phones, and Wi-Fi.

Work

I HAVE AN early shift at the Aloha Angel Cafe. When I hear the alarm go off at five thirty, my laptop is on the ground. It is the window to Umberto's travels. We talked until deep in the night—his body in the hospital and me on another island. He told me about his three faithful dogs from childhood that are now forever young in the garden.

He told me about the pain in his body in the hospital and how he can hover above it, but he doesn't want to go inside. He told me about his brother sitting next to his bed and his intimate thoughts, already anticipating that Umberto will die. He told me about visits to different places he has been in his life, like Jayapura, South Africa, and other places he has lived. He told me about visiting another realm with no shadows and meeting angels. He told me about Karen and how she moved on and was replaced by another guide who calls himself holy. At first, Karen asked Umberto to visit her parents in Minnesota to tell them that their daughter is okay.

"So, you are going to be back in your body then for that?" I teased him.

Underneath it all, there seems to be this unshakeable knowledge in him that he will come back to life. My connection with him seems to bypass all my fear for his death too. I am so impressed by the pace in which he seems to move from one state to the other.

***

"That's it!" I yell while passing the plumeria farm on Napoopoo Road at six o'clock with all its bare brown trees and pink and white flowers. "That's it." I hit my hand on the wheel of my old silver Subaru, which finds it harder every day to climb up the hill. "Umberto is a delog!"

It suddenly all comes back: the smell of butter tea, the simple little room next to the monastery, the Tibetan prints on the curtains, Jhampa's soft fingers reading my pulse, his mysterious sister Djawa, and all those afternoons in the monsoon rain. I had totally forgotten about it, but now I clearly remember those intimate moments with Jhampa in Dharamsala. How he told me about delogs visiting the other side, roaming around in other realms while their bodies are dead or in comas.

Umberto is a delog too! Even though he is not dead, he is in a coma. He is doing the same thing. I burst out laughing. Instead of consciously leaving his body, he just seems to get kicked out of it. He walks around like Alice in Wonderland. He is able to go wherever he puts his attention. Umberto is a modern delog, using modern technology to communicate to me. I am the witness on the other side. Just like that message announced to me, I can follow each move through my computer screen.

At the fork in the road, the corner with Keei Road, a couple is hitchhiking. The guy is really tall, and the girl is exceptionally short. They look like they are not from here, with their rainbow-colored clothing. Hoping that my car will make it up the rest of the hill, I let them step in. "You guys are early."

"Yes, we want to enjoy the day," she says with a slow smile. Her eyes the biggest and bluest I have ever seen. Everything about this couple seems slow. I regret stopping. I might be late for work since it takes them so long to put their entire luggage in the back of my car.

Still so full with everything that happened last night I blurt it out, as soon as I drive away: "Umberto—, my former lover on another island— fell into a coma yesterday and started to communicate to me on the computer, in handwritten letters. He wrote me from where he is, and I could type back. We talked for hours." I finish triumphantly, and I look at them, waiting for a response.

I don't know what I was expecting—at least some shock, surprise, or amazement.

"That is so cool," they say almost at the same time, both smiling. A strong patchouli smell surrounds them. There is no disbelief, skepticism, questioning, or verifying. I look at the road and then back at the mirror while I squeeze the wheel. I peer at their rainbow shawls, their earrings, their shirts, and their smiling faces.

My excitement turns into disappointment, and my disappointment turns into a slight anger. *Why don't you want to ask me questions? Why do you have no doubt about what I am saying? Why don't you want to see it with your own eyes? Why are you not questioning me?* I am amazed by my own need for validation. I need to have my doubts challenged, position myself, and choose one color instead of a whole rainbow. I want just somebody, anybody, to say: "Did that really happen?" So that I could say: "Yes, that did really happen." I want to say it out loud to convince myself.

The ride is short. When I drop them off across from the theater, I am glad to see the waitress who showed me the way on my first day at the Aloha Angel Cafe. Seeing Maureen seems to make everything more normal. I take a deep breath. She is tall and has big red curly hair and green eyes. I thought of her as a real angel from the first time I came to the restaurant.

"How are you?" she says.

I can feel her sincerity. *Not at my work. I am not going to tell it anybody at my work.* I had promised myself this. But I can feel it already pressing behind my eyes: tears, which I didn't even know that were there. Now it just comes out of me again: everything that happened—, even that Umberto died before. We now both step in the little hallway.

To my surprise, Maureen falls on the ground before me on her knees. Her head down, hands folded together.

"Let me pray for you and for Umberto," she says while she starts reciting something what seems like she has been rehearsing for days. "Oh, Lord please ... in the name of Jesus." It goes on and on and on, right on the dirty black mat of the workers' entrance, between stacks of bottles of beer and wine.

My tears have stopped. *Come on. Stand up. You don't need to pray for us. We are absolutely fine. Umberto is a delog and will find his way back.* Instead of telling her this, I just stand there, above her, embarrassed when more workers come inside. They give me a look, and I feel an incredible laughter rising. For one moment, I wish that my friends in Holland could see me. I long for them to see me like this and ask, "Did that really happen?" I could say from the bottom of my heart. "Yes, that did really happen." And that would be it. It would be better than Christians begging Jesus for help, spaced-out rainbow hippies, or Sixth Sense teachers telling me that it is not possible—as they would do later that night.

101

When I get home from work that afternoon, I call the hospital again. There is no new information. He is still in a coma, and there is no urge in me to go see him. I decide to sit down and say hello to him intuitively like we have learned at the center.

My laptop is on my bed. I close my eyes and try to see him in my mind's eye. I look at the keyboard, and my fingers want to touch it. *Shall I dare to try to contact him from this side? Will I disturb him?* So far, he only contacted me. *How will it be if I make the first move?*

I look at the tiny little Yahoo box. The rest of the screen just has my desktop picture on it: the picture of Kealakekua Bay, no black screen, and no sign of him contacting me. I open my email, to see if there is a message from his aunt. But there is nothing. I look at my fingers, my flexible, long Qigong fingers, and stretch them a few times. I take a deep breath.

And right at that moment, it happens again: the screen starts to vibrate and turns black.

The handwritten letters appear again: "Did you call me? I could hear your voice."

You could hear my voice? And I was only thinking about you? Not even typing? For a moment, I realize the power of "saying hello." I cannot wait to tell the Sixth Sense Center about it tonight.

He could hear me telepathically.

"Yes, I tried to say hello."

"I smell Organza."

"Really? Organza?" I burst out laughing. That perfume I once bought at a layover in London? I had only worn it twice when I was with him. I don't like artificial scents at all, but I liked the name, like an orgasm extravaganza.

"Every time when I am here in the garden, I can smell you as plumeria, and at other moments, I can smell you as organza. First I smell you, and then it makes me think about you—and I can hear your voice."

There is enough familiarity between us to connect, at the same time enough distance to not want to save him, to run over to go see his body, to feel too attached, or want to have him near me. After all, a whole ocean and an expensive trip separates us. And I am tethered to my job.

The blackness of my computer screen, the whole screen black, makes it more real to me. It is like he is writing on a blackboard in front of me.

The letters I type in the Yahoo Messenger box look way smaller than his handwritten letters in white, without frames or windows. This strange discrepancy bypasses my doubt. There is something about the black and white; the black reminds me of his dark skin, the dark water of the Ala Wai Canal, or the shadow that seemed to surround him.

"Umberto, you are a delog," I type in excitement. But the letters seem to bounce off an invisible wall.

"A what? Oh, Christel, where am I? The holy guide takes me somewhere. Are you still there with me?"

"Yes, I am here." It is almost as if I can feel him being pulled away, out of the garden.

"We are in an apartment building, Christel. The guide tells me we are in New York; he is pointing at what is taking place in front of us. 'Watch,' he says. He is pointing at a couple in front of us. I wonder why we are here; it is strange that they don't see us. They are at a table and seem to just have finished breakfast. They seem so happy together. She has red hair, freckles, and a beautiful face. She must be about thirty-five, our age. He is a little stocky with dark hair; he looks Italian and is just a little older. They look so in love. It is as if they finally found each other after many failed relationships. It's strange that I just know these things. 'Watch,' the guide says again. He seems to know everything already. We are standing right next to the table."

The letters appear on my screen rather quickly. I have to keep up with them; otherwise they will disappear off my screen forever. This focused attention somehow keeps me very close to him. I feel like I am right there with him, almost like a Peeping Tom. I try to imagine him whispering to me in this intimate moment that I am part of too.

"The woman starts to talk, taking his hand in hers. She says she has to tell him something. They have known each other for six months, and she has to tell him her secret. I feel uncomfortable, Christel."

"Me too," I type back, almost afraid that the couple will hear me. It feels so real. I can feel his discomfort, like a rumble in my belly, yet I am glued to the screen. "Umberto is a witness of complete strangers, and I am witnessing him!" I yell and put my hand in front of my mouth to not disturb anything. It is just another layer of the many things he is encountering.

He says, "The woman is saying, 'I think that now is a good moment to tell you about my secret.' 'Secret?' The man is lifting his eyebrows. She looks at him triumphantly while she is reaching into her red big bush of hair. Oh, Christel, no. In one move, she takes off the whole bunch of hair from her head. She is bald! 'I have a wig,' she says. 'My hair fell out years ago and never came back.' She says something about a strange disease. Oh no. His face is becoming pale and angry. He slashes his hands in the air. He is beating her. She is falling on the ground and yelling in rage. She is getting up, grabbing some stuff, and running out the door, leaving him in fury. I yell at him, but he cannot hear me."

"Oh, where am I now? I am back at the garden. Why am I screaming? Why am I here? Christel, are you still there?"

"Yes, I am still here. I followed everything."

"It is so confronting, Christel. Looking at this couple feels like I am looking at myself. I am exactly like that man. I can get so angry too. I can still feel it in my heart. It hurts so much. It is just like I was looking at myself. This guy is so attached to form, to how it is supposed to be, that everything different kills the love. He was so afraid of what others might think. It actually was the most beautiful thing: She was so vulnerable and innocent. They were so in love, and I just wanted to yell at him. You know what the guide says? 'It is not up to us to interfere with the process of the other. Everybody has to experience it for himself. It is up to them what they do with it.' He tells me that I am starting to face things in me, that they will immediately reflect in my body. I need to rest for a while to recover. That is why I am here. I am happy that I can talk to you, Christel."

It is just like I am in the garden with him. I can see him sitting there in his blue jeans and white shirt.

"I am so tired, Christel."

"Tired? Sleep well then … but you were asleep already. Remember?" I chuckle while I type the letters. How can you say sleep well to somebody already in a coma? The letters begin to fade on my screen. The black background vibrates, and my desktop picture emerges. The clock in the corner is visible again. It is almost six o'clock. Oh, no, I have to be at the Sixth Sense Center in thirty minutes. I cannot wait to tell them everything about it.

The Class

"NO. COMING BACK from death is not possible." Tina, the Sixth Sense teacher, peers at me with a firmness that almost blows me off my chair.

We are sitting with five students in a circle in the little air-conditioned room across from the ocean. Full of enthusiasm, I have just told everybody what I am experiencing. They all look at me with wide eyes and utter attention.

Jonathan started to clap in excitement.

Tina laughs her high obnoxious laugh. "Yes, of course you can have a near-death experience, but the body …"

I fade out for a minute.

Tina says, "We never try to connect to disembodied beings."

I cannot follow her anymore. Her words echo in my mind. I feel hammered down on top of my head. I felt so vulnerable, but I was excited to share my experience. The only person I had told about it was Tammy.

"Everything we talk about in this school is about the realization that we are a spirit and have a body. This is the proof," she exclaimed.

"Exactly," I said.

Helplessly, I look around the room, the others now feel like strangers. Tina, the teacher I admired before, Jonathan his blue eyes now glued on Tina. Julius who I started to like, looks serious again. Even Tammy who is sitting next to me and became a friend is looking at me as if I am an apostate. We are invited here over and over again "to look at the truth for ourselves" but that now seems lifetimes away.

"Yes, but … *it did really happen*," I want to say but now I even I start to doubt myself. Maybe it is wrong. Maybe it didn't really happen. Like even

Lennard, my always refreshing husband Lennard doesn't want to believe me. He doesn't believe in Umberto in the first place.

"All right. Let's breathe all this confusion out of our bodies," Tina says.

I cannot hear her anymore. I can only hear my nervous blood pumping in my ears. These stupid plastic chairs always disgust me. Why don't they just have a decent wooden chair like we have in Holland?

Dead

I HAD NEVER seen somebody in a coma until I was twenty-six and Shen took me as a student to see his Chinese friend, in a nursing home in Maastricht. His friend Wang owned a Chinese antique shop, and after a failed gallbladder operation, he had entered a coma. He lay lifeless on rhythmically pumping machines: a big body, a pale face. Colorless actually, or maybe it was the yellow hue over his whole body, because of his gallbladder that makes him look like he was made out of wax. A strange lurid scent lingered in the room. I wondered if it was the smell of death.

As soon as Shen came into the room, the man started to move vigorously, his whole body shook wildly; it was as if somebody had jiggled his bed. I couldn't believe my eyes at first. I knew about Shen's strong powers to create spontaneous movements, "empty force" he calls it, but not in a lifeless man. Shen gestured for me to come in.

"Here I show you how to treat somebody in a coma." He started waving his hands forcefully above the man's head. With squinting eyes, he looked at his face. Now he made movements towards his head, with his fingers he pointed at his crown as if saying, "there, there is the entrance."

"He doesn't want to be in his body, he just keeps floating above it, sulking," Shen muttered.

Every once in a while, Wang's body shook. Sometimes it was only the extremities, and at other times, his whole body shook like jelly. Shen pointed at his palm. I saw white, red, purple, and bluish cloudlike spots. The *binqi*, the sick energy, represented his anger.

"There is so much anger in his body," said Shen. "He is angry with his son, his wife, and everybody in his business. He is angry and feels incapable. They already accepted that he is going to die. His wife wishes him dead, and his son is just a hopeless layabout in his eyes. His anger keeps him stuck in this unconscious mist."

At that moment, the nurse came in ready to end our visit.

"Don't give him so much nutrition," Shen said, pointing at the tubes with the yellow gooey stuff entering his veins.

She didn't respond.

As she left the room, he told me that the liquid food was slowing down Wang's ability to come back in his body. "He is so frustrated that he is not able to communicate it to the nurse since he is right here, standing next to her and trying to yell it in her ear."

I could see a flash above his head. "Look. He is trying to enter his body."

Shen was wildly gesturing, waving above the guy's head, and then he stopped and looked at me. "One day, you will be doing this."

The words lingered in my mind. Shen had said so many things out of the blue that became true at some point.

Four months later, Wang woke up from his coma.

***

I haven't told anybody at the Aloha Angel café about it after I told Maureen. The only one I really trust is the cook: Paul is half Hawaiian and half Japanese with a yellowish face and gray, straight hair mostly in front of his eyes. He mixes a good sense of humor with a tremendous knowledge about Hawaiians. His laugh sometimes scares me; he laughs so hard with so much force that it is like one of his sharp knives coming down. But he feels like the safest to tell it to. So I did today.

I was nervous, standing in front of the kitchen counter right after the others had left already. I just had to tell it somebody. I told him all about Umberto on Oahu, about his death before and his coma now and our extraordinary communications on my laptop. It felt like too much at first and made me think about his sharp knives and his ability to use them like a samurai.

Paul looked at me, through his grey hair, scanning me. The sweat from the hot sultry kitchen was seeping down his upper chest like yellow pearls. Then he threw his hair to the side and commanded: "Tell me!"

Somewhat relieved I told him about the garden, about Umberto's travels, about heaven, the cancer in his body and then I talked about what just happened this morning, how Umberto first felt pulled into different directions, hearing all these voices, and feeling very confused. Forty-one dark creatures appeared, I don't know why it was forty-one, but they all wanted him; they are the Hawaiian spirits from the protection that his mother had put around him when he was nine. He said he beat a few of them in a heavy battle this morning.

It is silent for a while, I can see Paul swallow, then he bends over to me, over the greasy kitchen counter, and whispers: "I believe you, I know about these spirit warriors myself. It is real, Christel, very real." Then he turns his back toward me, and slams his knife on the cutting board. He looks back at me one more time. "They made *me* go to prison."

I call the hospital right after work, but there is no change in his physical body. The reality of his body seems to fade to the background quickly. My conversation with Paul is still with me—the strange mix of finally finding somebody who doesn't judge, is too gullible, or starts praying. A strange darkness came over us as Paul revealed his past.

When I get home, I decide I want nothing to do with those spirit warriors. I don't want to fight those dark vampires. I want to sit under a palm tree, be in nature, and take a refreshing swim in the quiet, deep blue ocean in front of the house. I run up to my bedroom and put on my bathing suit, which is still wet from yesterday.

Just then, my laptop makes the familiar pling sound announcing it received a message.

Is that Aran or his family? They would inform me through instant messaging if anything changed since they cannot call me on my phone without reception. There is no message or e-mail. "Umberto appears to be offline," the Yahoo box says.

My conversation with him is still visible from this morning. I hadn't even closed my laptop. Curiously I hop on the bed, my wet bathing suit in my hand, my body naked. I see the screen vibrate and become black. For the first time, I feel reluctant to talk to him, I long to go outside. A slight smell of his musty clothes mixed with laundry soap enters my nostrils as if I am smelling Umberto, just like he can smell me. It instantly makes me feel connected, not so much in a good way, or bad way either, but just connected.

109

"Christel, are you there? Where am I? I am in a room. There are no doors or windows. I am locked in here. Why am I here? I want to get out. Oh no. The light goes out. It is so dark, pitch-dark. Christel, are you there? Help me, Christel. Help!"

The letters jump off the screen like shrimp in boiling water. For the first time since we started communicating, I feel his desperate attempt to connect with me. It is like energetic arms trying to grab me. My desire to go outside and detach from his darkness and his neediness grows stronger. It's the same despondency I felt when we were still together, which made me want to move on.

"There is always light, Umberto, there is always light, there is the light in you," I can feel my impatience with the victim he now appears to be in a strange tension under my fingernails. Then for a moment, I look at the letters I just wrote: like it has happened a few times now—, almost as if it is dictated to me.

To my surprise, the hint of musty smell of his clothes seems to merge into the scent of night-blooming jasmine and my whole bedroom lightens up. Soda bubbles gush through my veins. For a moment, gravity disappears and I get a sense I am going to be lifted off of my bed any moment.

"That is so weird, it seems like I am experiencing it with him," I whisper loud and strong, squeezing my arms.

"Umberto?" I type.

"I am in the light! I just entered heaven, Christel, can you still hear me?"

***

For one whole day after this, Umberto's heart stopped beating, his breathing stopped. He was declared dead by the doctor. They were ready to bring him to the morgue. His Aunty Moana and his brother Aran left a whole row of voice messages on my phone, and they insisted to the doctors that they shouldn't bring him to the morgue. They had to sign a paper again that waived his death certificate they told me.

They didn't bring him to the morgue for one whole day. I called the hospital again; they wouldn't tell me he had passed away. If it weren't for the incredible experience of being lifted up with him, I wouldn't have believed his family when they said he had died again. Now it was undeniable.

And then … Umberto woke up. Our communications had continued while he was dead as if nothing really had changed. Seamlessly he slipped through a veil; first, there was the overwhelming homecoming, again the reunion with his family, an ultimate bliss, and then his journey just continued. His life on the other side just continued. Nothing really had changed.

When he finally started breathing again and his heart started pumping, I couldn't wait to go see him, despite my ambivalence. I wanted to see him with my own eyes again—to see the proof of his operation. Just to make it more real.

The Wound

IT HAS BEEN two weeks already. I couldn't come earlier. I could only come one day. I went back and forth from the Big Island to be with him for three hours before my return flight. I wanted to see him again for a little bit, put my nose in the creases of his neck, squeeze his dark skin deprived of blood for a whole day, and put my ear on his chest to hear his heart beat again. I wanted to feel his body, his aliveness next to mine, to make it all real again.

I throw my bag in the corner and let myself fall on the bed. "Show it to me!"

Umberto pulls up his shirt. Totally wrapped up.

"Can you take it off? Just for a little bit?"

"No, I can't, the doctor said."

"Hey, please?"

"Okay then." Carefully, he pulls on the bandage. A huge gash in his flank appears, embroidered neatly closed.

I swallow. The gash that opened his body: the whole other side of the operation that he had. I hadn't thought about anything besides the garden, the dogs, the scent, and his travels through the window of my laptop. I am sitting next to him on the bed in the house he shares with four other Indonesians—in his tasteless room with the smell of Indonesian food.

He puts back the bandage and then puts his pale blue shirt over it.

"It heals well," he hums.

"Why don't you look happy?" I poke him in his side and want to push him back on the bed. I want to lie on top of him with my little red dress, but he braces himself firmly.

"What is the matter?"

He shakes his head and stares at the gray carpet underneath him.

"There has been a new checkup, and I just got the results yesterday. There is more cancer in my lung. I have to have a new operation."

"No…" Like a pierced balloon, I feel the words deflate me.

"I don't know when exactly." He is quiet for a moment. "The doctor said when I woke up that he had never experienced something like this in his forty-year career. He said this is world news. This should be on television and in all newspapers. But I am happy that it didn't happen—, all that attention. I don't feel well at all right now."

"Why wasn't it on all the front pages?"

"It has to do with confidentiality. My aunt had to sign a paper to dismiss the death certificate they already made. The truth is that they are scared that we will sue them, because they declared me dead already. Now the whole thing is all hushed up," he mumbles.

"My God, what a hypocrisy, they should have given you a new birth certificate instead!" I stand up and pace up and down his room.

The cold, mechanical world of the hospital seems so far away: the medical procedures, drugs, insurance, doctors with their protocols and death certificates, and the industry of it all. Only the huge gash in his flank reminds us of the incision, the incision in his meat, his lung, his life. All closed neatly with needle and thread. Everything underneath it professionally covered up.

I could go to the hospital now—it is only a short bus ride away—and shake them up, ask for his paperwork, and confront them with the miracle, but there is only an hour left together. And soon Umberto will be under their wing again.

I feel my breath tightening as I get a strange sense that going there will take away from what it all really is. It will squeeze all the "out of the box-ness" from it and put it back in neatly.

"Honestly, you don't really look like a wonder of the world." I chuckle softly as I pace through the room.

Tears are dripping from his eyes. Faster and faster a whole chain of tears dripping down on the ground. I put my arm around him and smell that familiar smell with a hint of laundry soap of his shirt. "I think you are a delog," I try to say enthusiastically, and I explain what Jhampa once told me.

"Usually women, huh?" Umberto mumbles then shrugs his shoulders, like he would always shrug his shoulders indifferently. It has started to annoy me more and more. Just as we are getting to a point, it is hushed away. Just like the world news.

"Maybe it will help you with your healing to go to the Natural Healing Institute in Los Angeles. Lennard talks about it all the time. Terminally ill patients go there to cure themselves and get good results. I believe it is with colonics, fasting, a certain diet, and meditation or something. They have a whole program. They tackle the issue on different levels."

"Really?" He lifts his head and looks at me with his watery white-brown eyes.

"Yes."

"What was the name of it again?"

"Natural Healing Institute."

"Wait, I will write it down."

Angele

EVER SINCE I was young, I have had a strong attraction to my Aunt Angele. We spent many hours together after I turned eighteen and freedom was mine. She was the one I could tell about my sensitivities, my ability to move objects with my mind from a distance, my encounters with UFOs, my ability to talk to animals and flowers, my out-of-body experiences in the floatation tank, and my completely irrational intuitive choices. After all, she was a pioneer herself in her time. She liberated herself from the many limitations of the Catholic Church.

"Christel! How wonderful that you call me! And that all the way from Hawaii!" she says with excitement.

I sense a peculiar tension in her voice. Angele is the oldest sister of my father, and she still lives in Oisterwijk, in the south of Holland—only one street away from the house where I was born. It is a few weeks after I went to Honolulu to see Umberto, and I want to tell her about it. She has Parkinson's disease, which makes her body shake, but her mind is sharp as ever. Angele is my "spiritual mother." We are fifty years apart; she is the eldest, and I am the youngest in the family.

"Christel, I have had the most horrible night of my life. The maid who comes every morning just left, and everything just got cleaned up."

A weird sensation appears in my gut. "What happened?" I wish for a moment I was there with her. I spent so much time with her in my grandmother's house: with her little dogs, her lovely flower garden, and the blackbird singing on the roof. Her electric-blue eyes pierce through her platinum white hair, always in front of her eyes.

And she tells her story.

"I had to go pee in the middle of the night, like I always do at two

115

o'clock. This time, I woke up and could see two dark figures in my room. They were not physical but astral, but they were so present and real. They were holding my elbows behind my back. I couldn't go anywhere. I couldn't believe it at first, but I knew they were spirits. I usually have absolutely no respect for them. I just send them away, but they were so real and forceful. I could see every single one of them, and I couldn't believe how they were able to hold my body back. 'Let me go,' I shouted, but I couldn't move forward. Christel, it was horrible. They put a book in my head. It was the Bible! They tried to put the Bible in my head. It was so real, Christel. As you know, I have been confronted with that enough in my life already. They just kept on trying and trying. It was lasting for so long; ultimately, I fell to the ground. When I looked around, I saw all these dark men and women around me. All these spirits were sitting and praying with their hands in prayer position. I felt like I was in a church—a really big church. They all had dark skin and ugly grins. To make it even worse, I couldn't hold my pee anymore. I peed on the floor. I felt like I could cry. All of a sudden, it stopped. All of them vanished. I was exhausted. I fell asleep on the floor in my own pee. It was so horrendous. This morning, I heard the maid come inside. Thank God! She helped me. I have absolutely no clue how all this could have happened."

The church... praying... dark figures? Umberto? Oh no! My aunt's words seem amplified a thousand times in my head, echoing in all corners, louder and louder. I can feel the discomfort in my gut. *This must be Umberto. I am sure.* Her experience seems like an astral projection of what Umberto was talking about yesterday with the church and praying for others.

My phone conversation flashes in my mind. In order to make sense of it all, Umberto had told me on my short visit to Honolulu that he started talking to a pastor about his experiences. He never really went to church before, but his parents were devoted Christians. I didn't pay much attention to it right then, but the church took his experiences eagerly. They consider him a new prophet.

"I am now preaching in three different churches," he told me proudly. "Two Indonesian churches and one other one in Honolulu, and I was never even interested in church before."

I couldn't believe what he said. *You died and came back—and now you are going to limit your expansive experience to a church?* I told him I could imagine his need for a mentor. I told him about Shen and Aunt Angele. I mentioned that she was not doing well because of her Parkinson's disease, and it even might prevent her from staying in her house. That was Saturday afternoon, and now it is Sunday night.

"Oh, Angele!"

"And the worst thing, Christel, is that everybody has confirmation that it is irresponsible to leave me here in the house alone. I am really able to take care of myself. The last thing I want is to be evicted from this house." Her voice seems to fade to the background.

"Oh no!" I speak slowly.

"I feel good again. I am so glad you called! The Bible! They were trying to put the Bible in my head! Fortunately, they didn't succeed!"

"Yes, fortunately they couldn't!" I swallow and I can hear her soft familiar chuckle, the one I know so well from her in free and unlimited form.

I just have to call Umberto right now! I feel it in every pore when I hang up the conversation on Skype. He must be behind this. I listen to the phone ringing while I sit at my spot next to the ocean in the dark.

"Hey, how nice that you call me," Umberto says happily when he picks up the phone. And without any introduction he says: "We have prayed with the whole church for your aunt this morning; that must have been at least six hundred people. I wanted to pray for your aunt since you had just told me she was not doing well."

My breath stops for a moment. I cannot believe what I hear, the reality of it presented so clearly.

"It is really true!"

"I know," I answer.

"What do you mean?"

I tell Umberto the whole story, and he is quiet for a moment. I hold my breath. Did I say too much? Does he feel attacked? Does he see it as rejection? The fundamental difference between us is as clear as a knife slicing a white canvas, damaged forever.

"I would have never expected that, I am so, so sorry..." he mumbles. He is silent for a while. "Would it be okay, if I just talk straight to her?"

117

'Yes, just let him do that' the whisper urges me stronger than usual, and I know I can trust it. I feel its soft embrace touching on the backs of my hands.

I sigh deeply as a weight slides off my shoulders. I know he means that he is able to talk directly to her soul without the circus of the church. I learned to do the same thing at the Sixth Sense Center.

Here it is again, that strange feeling, this incredible energy. It is like a big wave that needs to be forced in a little ditch. On the one hand, Umberto has these incredible experiences, like a phoenix arising time after time. On the other hand, it seems like he is so afraid of it. He needs to put it into a system no matter what. Denying the free spirit he really is, he follows the system of the church and the rules of his ancestral lineage. Yet I so know he can free himself, if only he would choose. Like we all can. How he will now speak to the phoenix in Angele; Angele, the symbol of a free spirit to me.

***

The next morning, right when I arrive at the café, I'm surprised to receive a phone call from my father. He is twelve time zones away in the north of Holland, and he never calls me. In an excited voice, he tells me that the committee voted to let Angele stay in her house. She appears to be stronger than ever and can stay in the family home. "This is not what we expected," he says. I call Angele immediately, still standing in the little hallway of the theater.

"Remember, Angele, how I talked before about Umberto—the guy who died and came back?"

"Yes? Such a strange story, but knowing you, it's not a surprise," Angele says cheerfully.

"Well, he decided to pray for you with the whole Indonesian church. That's why you saw the dark skin. They are convinced they are doing something good, but they have absolutely no clue how it is for you since you hate the church."

"Really, Christel?" she says deeply and slowly and forcefully, as only she can. "Really? But how would you explain that I felt so good after and that the team wasn't able to prove that it is irresponsible to stay in my house?"

"Well, Umberto asked me if he could just talk straight to your spirit

118

without the whole circus of the church. I know he can. He knows how to fly. He just told me a story about how he talked to the spirit of a guy who just committed suicide by jumping off an overpass. He saw the man's spirit jump out of his body. Umberto was able to tell him about the choice for life or death; he is such a phoenix too. He felt so bad for you and couldn't believe it at first."

"Wow. At least something beautiful came out of it. It saved me from having to leave my lovely house!"

Yes, your house—your own ground and your own truth.

Mock-Up

THERE IS ONE day in the forty-nine days I spent with Umberto in Waikiki that stands out way above all the other days. At the Sixth Sense Center, they call a template for what you want to create a "mock-up."

Umberto and I made a mega-mock-up. It was in the week before I moved back to the Big Island. That day seemed to be of a totally different order. We were at Sans Souci Beach. I dove in the water and somersaulted down and so did he. In the clear underwater world, we found each other's hands. The bubbles that came out of his smiling mouth surrounded our faces. The water changed from monotonous blue to reflecting a thousand dimensions more as we came to the surface. Then everything seemed to be saturated with life force.

This is why I met Umberto, I thought in a flash. It was so the opposite from the dark water of the Ala Wai Canal on the other side of Waikiki when we met. There was Umberto's smiling face. The blue shades reflected by the water were audible, and the sun was dazzling. Everything was shiny and lucent as in a Technicolor movie. I looked deep into his mysterious eyes, our chins still under water.

And then he said it, without any introduction: "Anything is possible." And he said it with so much spark and so much authority. It was unlike anything else I ever heard from him.

I absorbed his words and said, "Anything is possible."

We kept repeating it. In the background, I could hear my mind trying to understand. I struggled to find similar experiences, explanations, or control, but I was unable to find any.

In images, the words became visible around me. Uncountable images bubbled out of us. A kaleidoscope of images—every piece in the kaleidoscope—was a world in itself. I saw Umberto in a blue hospital gown, a brown wooden house on a mountain, a green house next to a river, golden cogs of two wheels meeting, a baby, doctors, millions of books, an ambulance, golden music, colors, gardens with flowers and butterflies, cities with light, a dark wound, a lot of stairs spiraling up, a Hawaiian ceremony, oceans, cheering people, screaming people, and a computer screen.

Exactly the same computer screen I am looking at right now, brings back that memory. I received a message from Aunty Moana: "Emergency" it said. Umberto had the second lung operation and entered a coma.

Gold Gunk

WHEN I ENTER the thick glass sliding door of the Sixth Sense Center, Linda, the director, is already waiting for me. "Christel, I have to talk to you." She is as resolute and snappy as ever. She is wearing bright red lipstick, and her heels are extra high. I am still a head taller than she is. Her dark eyes seem to want to pierce through me.

"Hello, Linda. I have a class right now."

"I know, but it can wait. Tina knows that you will be a little late." Tina is the teacher today. "Follow me to my office."

She patters to a tiny yellow room that once was a bathroom. There are a few drawings of roses on the walls. My friend Julius told me that every rose represents a class. That makes it easier for the teachers to connect to the group and see what energies can be perceived in it. For example, they can intuitively see how a student in the group is affecting the energy of the whole class, bringing in disturbing energies like disbelief, atheist energy, or strong emotions.

The roses are perfectly positioned next to each other in three different rows. The first row must be the beginning clairvoyant classes. Each one is bigger than the one before it. They represent the energy of the growth period that a whole group is going through. The further along you are in the three-year program, the bigger your challenges are.

The first rose is a small blue one; it must be from the little group that started last week. A big pink rose catches my eye; there are some yellow spots around it. I intuitively know it represents our group. I am in the third year of the program, and I wonder what they actually do with the pictures. I try to concentrate on one, but Linda takes me out of my concentration and gestures me to sit down.

"All right," she starts. "I have heard from different teachers that you had such an *interesting* experience," she speaks mockingly. "Tell me about it?"

Hesitantly I start. But soon she interferes, sticks her hand up in the air, and turns her head away, like she is holding up traffic, showing me her long, black, shiny hair.

"This matter is not suitable for this place, too many students are disturbed by it—, without them even knowing it—, and it creates this 'un-safety' for them, so I am going to ask you now to keep your mouth shut." She turns her head back to me, piercing me with her dark eyes.

In Sixth Sense terms, they call it "being lit up." When readers are lit up, their bodies feel uncomfortable, tired, or sick before a class or a reading. It is an issue or a theme that wants to be addressed, looked in the eye, or expressed through the body. It is a good thing. We learn to not resist it or run away. We look at it and release the charge or energy around it so it can be seen for what it really is.

"Coming back from death is not possible, Christel. What we do here is keep the space clear and safe, these kinds of stories don't belong here."

"Yes, but ..." I try to look for words. *It really happened.* They always taught us to look the monster—the unknown—straight in the eyes. A big door shuts in front of me. The door is not able to open anymore. My mouth is gagged.

"It is time to go back to your class." Linda points at the door.

***

Here I am, the door shut already behind me. Aghast, I look around me, not a trace of warmth, or cordiality. *What am I doing here?* I look wishfully at the glass exit door. On the other side of the road, a slice of blue ocean is visible under the big green-red kamani tree. I face the middle door where my class has started. I open it carefully and sneak inside. A white plastic chair is waiting for me.

They all have their eyes closed. Tina smiles at me. I liked her at first, but ever since she disapproved of my experience, my affection has faded. She points out that I will be the space-holder today; the rest of the students will be doing the reading. A space-holder is like a beacon for the others who literally stands above it while the other students are sitting.

Moving around with the chairs, I see Christine and Sarah glance at

123

me. *Is it my imagination or are they really looking at me suspiciously? Did they talk about me in the group? Did they say that I do things that are not possible? Did they say I made it up?* I get up to stretch, and I am happy about my position today. I watch the others make two rows of chairs. I follow the familiar steps. I imagine that my crown is filled with golden light, and then I connect to my "knowingness," which brings me in my authority. I keep the space safe by visualizing everybody in a golden bubble. It is my task to see if any energy wants to enter that bubble or sabotage it. I have to keep it safe. I giggle at the idea that I am the one who makes everybody feel unsafe.

The readers are sitting in rows of four. Jeremy is in front of them and is being read. I feel confident today. For a moment, my thoughts return to my conversation with Linda. It doesn't seem to affect me anymore. My eyes scan the room. Sometimes I am able to see energy as a misty cloud or a flash around somebody's head. Other times, I just know that something is trying to interfere: a deceased ancestor, the church, an institution, or even a collective consciousness that wants to prevent us from taking steps toward independence or freedom. Sometimes it is like a slight pressure in the room—something that just doesn't feel right—but everything seems to be flawless today.

I scan the room again. My eyes land on my red leather handbag that I had thrown in a corner while rushing in. In a flash, it hits me. *Umberto is trying to reach me on the phone!* I know it for a fact. He is trying to reach me from his coma. The anxiousness turns into panic. My phone will start ringing any minute because I forgot to put it on vibrate! With all my focus, I try to concentrate on my cell phone. *Don't ring. Please don't ring.*

It occurs to me what an absurd thought it is that Umberto wants to reach me on my cell phone since he is in a coma. Reaching me on my laptop is one thing, but to think he is able to reach me through my cell phone seems ridiculous. I look around the room and panic. I cannot walk over to my bag because there is not enough space. What shall I do? All my concentration and my seniority is gone. The group seems to notice nothing at all. They are talking about the "havingness" of Jeremy, which is his ability to really hear what the readers have to say so he can make use of it. Everybody looks happy, which makes me even more frustrated.

"Now come back, everyone. Open your eyes and put the chairs back in a circle. Christel, sit here with us. You have done an excellent job keeping us all safe and clear."

Yes, but … I decide to keep it for myself. I almost lost it.

Tina looks around the room. "So, Jeremy, tell me …"

***

"Christel, are you there?"

"Yes, I am here. I just got home."

"I saw everything! You had to go to the director in that little room. I saw how she spoke to you and how you went into your classroom."

"Yes, that is right! Linda is the director. What do you think? Because of you!"

"And you know what? I tried to reach you in that classroom, but I couldn't. I tried to do everything to come close. Whatever I did, I wasn't able to. There was all this … hmmm, how would I call it … this stuff around you, a kind of a golden gunk, a liquid mass. It didn't let me get to you. It pushed me back each time. I got really irritated about it. You seemed to not notice at all. You were just standing there in that gold gunk."

My mouth opens from amazement. I can still see the letters appearing on the bottom of the screen. They are disappearing on the top, slipping away from my screen forever. *He saw it all? He saw exactly what I was doing? He saw me keeping the space safe from intruders? He saw it as golden gunk?* Amazing. That is exactly how I had imagined it. I visualized a golden gunk around the students. That is the job as a space-holder. What an incredible confirmation that it really works. I laugh. I had felt it exactly right! He was trying to reach me in whatever way he could. Apparently, I felt his panic and frustration in not being able to reach me.

"Well, I wasn't that stoic at all," I say. "I felt so nervous all of a sudden, and I was convinced that it had to do with you. I actually had the idea that you were trying to reach me on my cell phone!"

"Cell phone?"

I almost hear the surprise in his tone.

"Yes, you were trying to reach me on my phone—just like you communicate through the computer."

"Computer?"

"Yes, we communicate to each other through the computer, right?"

He doesn't seem to get that his words just appear on my screen as handwritten letters. For him, it seems like he is hearing my voice. Close or far away. Whispering, sweet or tired.

***

The excitement sizzles through my body. I want to tell Julius, Susanna, Christine, Sarah, Jeremy, Jonathan, Tammy, and all the other students and teachers. I want to tell them it really works! I really did create a golden bubble. Umberto can see it all from the other side!

He tells me that the golden gunk seems to change in structure. One moment, it is as liquid as water, and the next, it is sticky as syrup. The more he was trying to go through it to reach me, the more it seemed to prevent him from entering. When he was trying to enter it with a lot of force like a wild bull running into it, it was like a metal wall.

The golden gunk, the field I was creating around the group, seems to change according to the energy that is trying to get through, like a multifunctional shield. The way it is approached determines the experience. What a fantastic concept! Tomorrow night, I have another class. I could print out what he has told me so the proof is there. They can read it with their own eyes. I could put it on the bulletin board, and all the other classes could read it too. I could even put it on their website.

"They won't believe you. They will tell you that you made it all up."

Just like a slap in my face, the words appear on the screen, my head starts to whizz. *Umberto has read my mind.* He can see my enthusiasm and how I want to convince everybody about it. And the irony of it is that he is right. It all comes back: the frigid hand from Linda in that tiny room and the piercing eyes like a police officer. It all comes back and I now know it for a fact: All the students know about it. They are all informed that they shouldn't listen to my story and especially should not take it seriously.

***

Umberto stayed in a coma for two more days. Like every time so far, something profoundly changed after his return. The first time he stopped eating meat and started to visit all the *heiaus*, ancient sacred Hawaiian sites on all four corners of Oahu. He said his guide told him to do so.

The second time, he became hooked on the Indonesian church and started to preach, whereas he never went to church before. He also suddenly liked coffee, which he had always despised. And now, the third time after he wakes up out of a coma, it appears that the cancer in his lungs miraculously healed. To my surprise he wants to "do healthy." He wants to eat well, exercise, and meditate. He says he wants to go to the Natural Healing Institute in Los Angeles.

Butterfly

FINALLY, MY PERMANENT resident card arrives in the mail. I have permission to stay in Hawaii. After a year of not being able to leave the country, I decide to take a short trip to Holland to see my parents and some friends.

"Christel, look!" my mother calls me from the upstairs bathroom in my parent's house. I run up the wooden stairs my father made. "Have you ever seen a big butterfly like that? Have you ever? And in the winter!" She is in awe.

I swallow. I am back in Holland for two weeks. I am in my old bathroom with the white and green tiles from the seventies. I look out the window that I looked through so many times, and I see a big, black butterfly. I know Umberto is in a coma again. The butterfly is opening and closing its wings.

"Where did it come from? The door has not been open in weeks," my mother asks as it flutters against the little window.

For a moment, I am afraid she will crush it. I look closely at its pristine patterns. We study its refined, beautifully crafted, black lace wings. I wonder if I can tell her. Our heads rest together gently, her dyed reddish-brown hair against mine. If it were my father, it would have been easier. He understands without questions, but my mother just gets afraid.

***

On my way to Friesland, I stopped at an old friend's house. Ton's house is between fields and cows. I asked him if I could check my e-mail on his computer. That is where it happened. He went upstairs to make me some

128

coffee on his new machine. "I want to know everything about Hawaii," he yelled.

I sat alone in his downstairs bedroom at his big computer. As I was about to put in my password, the screen went black. I froze in my seat and pushed myself away from the table. For a second, the screen started to vibrate. I had gotten used to that—but not on somebody else's computer.

Umberto's smiling face appeared over the whole screen. It was so real, so close, and so present that I felt he could step out of it any moment. I was shocked. I knew he was not in his body. He was trying to connect and tell me something. We hadn't spoken for a while and had more or less said farewell to each other before continuing with our lives.

Ton walked in the door with his happy face, virile eyes, black curls, and steaming coffee.

"Are you okay? You look so pale. You must be tired."

My eyes stayed fixed on his screen. It had returned to normal. The sign-in window from my Hotmail account and the little blinking cursor were comforting. I exhaled deeply, trying to regain my composure. It was too fresh, too strange, and too close to acknowledge it for myself—let alone tell Ton. My heart was beating in my throat. I was so uncomfortable. Jittery blood was speeding through my body. I needed to get out of there. I wasn't sure if it was Umberto's thought or mine.

***

And now I am here with my mother, looking at this creature attached to Umberto.

"Wow. Look at it, Christel. It is so black and so big. It is so beautiful. Is it a moth or a butterfly?"

"A night butterfly," I hear myself say. *A night butterfly*. It echoes in me.

I had just considered it a coincidence. In the beginning, I hadn't even noticed the connection between his in-between state and my reality. I thought it was just a coincidence, but it became a pattern. Every time he was on the other side—whether he was in a coma or dead—I would see it. I saw it on the little flower on my way to the dolphins, on the roof of my car, inside my car, on the beach in Makalavena, and at the Choice Market in Captain Cook. Sometimes it was at night, and sometimes it was during the day. I saw it in the strangest places, opening and closing her wings.

She was tenderly sticking out her tentacles, fluttering in front of me, or touching my face.

Humans without bodies appear as animals. They hitchhike in butterflies, ladybugs, tiny bees, and big horses. They come and go. They attach to living beings. They attach to dragonflies, lizards, cats, dogs, and birds. They are shaman birds, cardinals, owls, swans, and even chickens. I don't know how they do it.

They attach and hitchhike. That is the way they communicate and make themselves visible.

I learned this from Umberto. Most of the time, I ignored the butterfly. It kept presenting itself to me. It showed up in the corners of my reality, in the corner of my eye, at the top of a palm tree, in front of a window, or inside the Sixth Sense Center. It even showed up in Holland—in a place where this size butterfly doesn't exist.

"What shall we do with it, Christel? It will freeze to death in the cold if we open the window."

"Let's put it in the attic. That is where it can sleep till winter is over." I smile about the metaphor of it all.

"Yes, that is where I see the little ones sometimes, waiting for the warmth." My mother grabs a towel and deftly puts it around its wings. For one moment, I feel the fear again that she will crush it, but she rushes to the attic.

I see it flutter away in the dark.

Cords

IT WAS WONDERFUL to be in Holland, connect to my friends and family again, and put things in perspective. My friend Grace, the astrologer, had even arranged for me to give a big lecture about my experiences with Umberto. I was eager to do so.

Finally, there was an audience who could ask, "Did that really happen?"

With all of my heart, I could say, "Yes, this did really happen."

The responses were overwhelming. The ones who knew me said, "We know you too well. We know that you wouldn't make this up."

The ones I didn't know gave me a standing ovation. It was as if they could feel the truth about delogs and their message. We have the ability to heal our bodies through our spirits. We can stand up against the power of the energetic tsunami.

On my return flight, I was finally ready to bring Layka, my five-year-old dog, to Hawaii. For months, I had been working on the paperwork because of the strict quarantine laws. Layka is my sweet Kooikerdog, a traditional Dutch breed that is still used in Holland to capture ducks. The dog seduces the ducks with his tail. They look like spaniels, red and white in color with long hair. They are famous for their intelligence and absolute loyalty. In Dutch history, a famous Kooikerdog saved the whole country by warning the governor Willem van Oranje about Spanish invaders in the middle of the night. The dog prevented an invasion.

Everything on the trip went smoothly. Twenty-four hours later, I stepped out of the plane in Kona with Layka. Over and over again, I had communicated to her telepathically about the big change, and she seemed to adjust well. My new life on the Big Island was even more complete; it felt like I had brought a piece of me with her.

"Tonight we are going to cut cords." Linda was sitting in front of the Sixth Sense students. It sounded like we were going to do some handcrafting or weaving. I imagined thick ropes; old ship ropes, frayed and weathered, like heavy weights. I pictured ropes with stories, history changed over time, feather-light thread, golden stardust woven together, and nourishing umbilical cords. I am looking forward to tonight; a whole new topic will be explored. We touch upon so many interesting topics. We are a group of seven, and Linda is going to explain cutting cords between people. I pair up with Carol, and Linda explains the steps. I study Carol's face; she has her eyes closed already.

"Okay, first, I will take a look at what kind of cords I see." I hold my breath and see Carol waving in the air with her hand. I cannot hear the others anymore.

A strange knot appears in my stomach. It is as if something is literally pulling on it.

A smile appears on Carol's face. She hasn't said a word, and I am starting to get a little uncomfortable. *What is she seeing?*

"I see something like a monkey," she starts. She describes how somebody, Umberto, is holding on to me energetically. He is helpless and caught in confusion. I feel responsible for him, she says, and that is my pattern. A lump appears in my throat. *Is it the resistance I somehow deep down started noticing when I was chatting with him, but had not yet acknowledged for myself? Do I feel responsible for him?*

When Carol opens her eyes for a moment, I see wonder on her face—or maybe it is worry. She knows the whole story. I can only nod; we don't have to give it words.

"See if you can exactly name who you are looking at," Linda says.

Carol is already way ahead. She is not saying much anymore, but I see her gesturing a lot. She strains her face, and it is as if I can read the disgust. The image from the heavy ship rope, returns. I close my eyes for a moment, but then I get dizzy and fall away.

"Keep your eyes open, Christel," I hear Linda say sternly in the background.

"Ask now for permission to cut the cord. This doesn't mean that the relationship will end, but that the foundation of it can change. As soon as there is love, there is connection—in whatever relationship it was."

I try to swallow the big lump.

Carol raises her clear, blue eyes for a moment, smiles, and repeats the question.

I nod and my thoughts wander to Umberto. He had decided to go to the Natural Healing Institute in Los Angeles. Maybe he is sitting in the Jacuzzi like he always does at the end of the day. After colonics, conversations about his behavior, and drinking juice, he spends every night in the Jacuzzi. I realized how relieved I was that he was taking charge of his own health; an update of the cord would be very appropriate. I wonder if it is possible to have another kind of relationship with him—not one in which I feel like a cheerleader cheering him to choose for life.

"Yes," I say out loud. "Yes. I want to cut the cord with Umberto." I notice a slight tremble in my voice when I pronounce his name. It is almost like a betrayal.

What happens now is so fast and so intense that I feel overwhelmed by it: a combination of big scissors cutting and something being pulled out of my gut. For a moment, everything becomes black. The floor appears to be a moving, watery surface. I see a hole—a wound still dripping from the fluid. I am gasping for air, and my head spins.

Carol still has her eyes closed. Her hands move as if she is pulling out the rest like long threads. I don't know if I feel relieved or not.

"Okay," Carol says. "Let's fill it up with your own energy."

Slowly, the ground underneath me becomes solid again. The whirlwind in my head fades, and the bleeding stops. I sigh and look around in the room. The presence of the group has totally eluded me. It is as if I was disconnected for a moment. I hear the harshness in the chattering of Linda's voice. It is hard, penetrating, and almost vitriolic. *Hmmm, strange how all of a sudden, I perceive things in a different way.*

"The place where the cord has been will need some time to heal," Linda says. "Give it space or somebody will just jump in exactly at the same place. We have cut a cord, and the convictions that a person was holding around the relationship are neutralized. That needs time to settle."

I see a few students nod. I sigh. I notice more space in my heart. Something is gone, and it feels like a little draft. I like it actually.

Alcohol

WITH A SHOCK, I wake up and sit up. I look around and pant. Sweat drips from my body as I pull away the sheets. My forehead, chest, and belly are soaked. My eyes try to adjust to the dark. Part of the room is brightened by the almost-full moon. For a moment, I see the silvery shine on the wooden floor. It looks so magical. I am in the middle of the dream again—a dream about Umberto. I never dreamed about him before, but now, it is so real. It is like I just landed in bed a second ago.

I saw him sitting in a room with only a chair and a bluish gleam around him. I almost didn't recognize him. His eyes were swollen and bulged out of their sockets. His body was swollen. He was shivering and covered in sweat. He looked at me with his big eyes. He looked helpless. I gestured for him to get up, but he didn't shift. He shook in that chair like he was glued to it.

A cool breeze enters the room. I look at the curtain moving and turn my head toward my laptop. *No, it cannot be. He is in the Natural Healing Institute, and everything appeared to be going so well.*

In a trance, I let myself slide off the bed. I click the light and grab my laptop. The startup is slow. I walk to the window and look outside. My right hand grasps my chest in the place where the cord was removed last night. It still feels fragile and vulnerable. The ocean looks wild: waves crashing violently on the black lava rocks and swirling white foam reflecting the moonlight. A chill runs down my spine, and I walk to my closet to get a vest on this warm summer night.

Pling. A message appears in the little Yahoo box. "Christel, are you there?"

"Umberto, what is the matter. Where are you?"

The chills become stronger. An image from last night comes back in my mind: the thick ship rope that was pulled out of my heart.

"It is Aran. Umberto is in a coma."

"A coma? Again? Can I call you on the phone?"

"Yes, please call me on Umberto's phone. It is early morning here." I run across the street to get cell phone reception.

Aran is a professional photographer, and his voice is so different than Umberto's. It is so much more sophisticated. "It is very strange," he says. "Umberto had an alcohol overdose. Last night, he called his friends from when he lived in Los Angeles. He suggested that they all go to a bar. His friends came to get him and told him that he was not supposed to have alcohol. He said, 'I don't care.' He got so drunk. We were dumbstruck because he was supposed to be at the institute—and he never drinks. He started to vomit, and blood came out of his mouth. A few minutes later, he was unconscious. We are at the hospital."

"But I talked with him every day last week, and he was so enthusiastic about the treatment, the colonics, the classes, and the diet. He was so proud of himself!"

In a flash, I see the thick ship's rope.

"He drank two bottles of vodka and half a bottle of Chivas Regal. His liver almost exploded. A little more, and he would have been dead. His kidneys are very badly damaged. They said there was so much alcohol in his body that they were not able to give him any medicine. He kept on saying to Uncle Ryan, 'No connection, no more connection. I hate this connection.' We didn't understand it."

I stare at the phone. *No more connection? The cord that is cut.* He must have felt it *literally.* I can hear blood pumping in my ears. It is almost as loud as the crashing of the waves in front of me. I see the dream again. I close my eyes and try to see him again on that chair in that empty blue room. In my mind, I say hello to him. I run back to the house and open my laptop. The screen starts to vibrate, but it doesn't turn black. The desktop picture of the ocean remains. For the first time, the handwritten letters appear in the Yahoo Messenger window. *Can I trust this? These letters are not straight across my screen. They are not white.*

"Why do you hate me?" The handwriting appears.

Is he trying to manipulate me? Is this still Aran?

"Why do you hate me?"

I look at the Yahoo messenger box; the letters are smaller and in black. It is so much grimmer than before. He must have caught my thoughts that I was trying to connect to him.

I feel a lump in my throat—the same lump I felt last night. A slight guilt seeps out of it. The words enter the wound in my heart as if salt is thrown into it. *Hate?* "Hate is not being able to feel love." Carol's words echo in my mind.

I look around me: next to the bed a little statue with two dolphins wrapped around each other grabs my attention, it makes me feel the love for everything as I know him, his origins so carved in his dark face, his shark-like wildness hidden in his eyes, the mumbling through his big lips, keeping it all inside. His posture is so weighed down by something unknown, something so big, impossible to carry.

"Why did you call me?" his message continues.

"I saw you sitting in isolation on a chair in an empty room in a dream. I wanted to say hello to you. It was just so real," I type cautiously.

"I like it where I am right now. There is no pain or sadness here. I hear so many voices; it is so confusing. I see so many people around me. They look so scary, and they want to take me to a scary, dark place. Why you hate me, Christel?"

A strange cold envelops me. I wrap my arms around my knees. I feel so far from him right now, and the wound in my heart squeezes. I stare at the letters on my screen. *Do I feel what he is going through right now?* I don't want it anymore—not any of it. I don't want to be a witness to Umberto's travels. I don't want to talk. I don't want him to jump back in my heart like Linda said could happen after the cutting of the cord.

In my mind's eye, I see him floating around in confusion. He in the "near-earth realms: as Jhampa would say, a victim of the voices. It is like the voices of the tsunami that were calling him before. For the first time, I don't feel the urge to tell him he can still choose. I am too detached from him. I squeeze my hands into fists when I think about the Sixth Sense Center.

If only I could tell them about the reality of it as it unfolds in front of my eyes. The reality of cutting the cord is reflected in our conversation, but there is no permission. If only I could tell them about all the phases

Umberto is going through, all those different layers, and the body's reflection of his soul's journey on the other side. I am a witness, and he is connected to a collective consciousness.

A week ago, he predicted a catastrophic storm on my computer screen. Two days ago, Hurricane Katrina hit New Orleans.

Keys

"YOU NEED A new car," Lennard had said when my Subaru broke down. He was on a short visit. As with everything with Lennard, it was so said and done: a friendly man at the dealership and a loan in Lennard's name. I would pay him each month—and never be late—and I had a brand- new four-wheel-drive Toyota Highlander. It was perfect for my upcoming retreats.

On our drive home, I tell him about everything that happened with Umberto. He is not very impressed with him, but he never was. Lennard never really approved of Umberto, and my experience doesn't really change it. He saw Umberto now a few times in Waikiki. He had a Bible under his arm and was on his way to church.

I sighed and tried to convince him. I looked at Lennard's freshly styled hair, his shiny face, his happy eyes, his skinny long legs in his bright shorts, and I surrendered to his "up-ness." He was ready for a new adventure. He had been the advocate for all the upgrades in my life: my permanent residency, a new laptop, and a new car.

***

I awake to a rumbling in my bag on the floor next to the bed. Is it my imagination? It sounds as if somebody is shaking my new keychain. *My keys from my new Toyota?* I sit up straight, and the rumbling in the bag stops. A weak moonlight enters the room. *I see my car keys floating in the air.* They are hanging as if an invisible hand is holding them. I am breathless for a moment.

I start to breathe forcefully. The keys drop onto my bed. *It must be Umberto.* His body is still in the hospital in Los Angeles. He has been

138

there for almost a week, moving in and out of his body and crossing many realities. We have hardly communicated this time; after the cutting of the cord, everything seems to have changed.

His brother keeps me updated through e-mail about his changes. His heart stopped for a while yesterday, and I haven't heard from them since. For me, there seems to be almost no difference whether he is in a coma or crossing over to death.

Squeezing my eyes, I try to see him. I try to perceive his shape. A dark silhouette? My eyes are pulled toward Layka on the mat by the door. She is sitting up and staring into the void without making a sound. For a moment, she lifts her tail—and then she quickly tucks it tightly around her legs. *Umberto? This must be Umberto. I know it for sure!*

I reach toward my keys. I am afraid to touch them. *Will I be able to feel something? Smell it maybe? Will there be a difference in temperature? Is the key a gate to a magical world?*

Layka is still looking into the void.

"Umberto," I say anxiously. "Do it again!"

Even before my laptop has completely started up, a message appears. "Beautiful car you have. I didn't want to scare you. Were you able to see me? I was standing at the end of your bed."

"No. I am not able to see you. I could only see the keys moving through the air. With all my imagination, I tried to see you, but I couldn't. For a second, I thought I saw a dark shadow, but then I realized I was just hoping to see it."

"Layka did see me though! You know why I was shaking your keys? I know that I will be back and will sit next to you in that car."

I feel my blood almost coming to a stop. It feels like ants crawling backward. *What if that is the last thing I want?*

My life starts to slowly fall apart. I cannot talk about it at my work, Lennard doesn't want to hear it, and even the Sixth Sense Center is not open. Only my friends in Holland believe me. Anger rushes through my body like a flooding river. *Is it because of the broken cord that I can feel my own point of view so vividly?*

"The guide that calls himself holy told me that I would cross over again. He didn't say how, but he prepared me. He just said it was not because of cancer."

"So then you thought you could just drink yourself to death?"

I don't want to be the reason for his existence anymore. I have no place for him, in my car or in my life. After his turn toward the church and the episode with Angele, my feelings for him changed so much. I can sense his not choosing.

I gaze at my keys. I pick them up carefully and imagine myself radiantly driving my new strong car over the island—straight across the lava with the wind in my face. I feel the freedom. What a coincidence. I break the cord with Umberto and promptly get the keys to my new car-my new freedom.

***

The next morning, I chuckle as I turn the key in my new car, – the key that floated in the air last night – and hear the mighty sound of the horsepowerengine roar.

It is busy on the road today, and I cannot wait to come out of this slow snake of vehicles. I sigh impatiently. In a while, I will be able to push the pedal with my foot again. It is so wonderful to be so much higher than in my little Subaru and I have a totally different view on the world. When I look to the left, I can see the white letters in the coral contrasting with the black lava. It brings good luck they say. Hundreds of people have written their names here with little pieces of white coral from a nearby beach. Like a black and white pen drawing, the white letters contrast the black surface.

At the end of the area against a little hill, I see my name. It is surrounded by a few other Dutch names that we put there during a retreat. Untouched by wind or weather, the coral just sits there. For the very first time, I can see my whole name from the road. With my Subaru, I could never see the "el." I could only see "Christ." The rest of my name means divine, I was once told. The traffic is stuck today. The "c" is a little smaller than I wanted it to be. The warm black lava sizzles underneath. I feel pulsing in my belly as I look at it.

I secretly despised my name my whole life because it sounded so much like *Christian* in Dutch. I always had the thought that people would associate me with Christianity, which equals *prude* to me. What a joy that, all of a sudden, my name was pronounced as "Crystal." For the first time, coming out of the mouth of a customs officer, "Welcome to the

140

United States, Crystal." I felt like I finally was seen for who I was—in this land with another language. In the first few weeks, when my name was pronounced like that, my heart leaped. My name was so much more alive and vibrant. Away with the Christian prudeness!

Exalted I turn left and turn unto the lava rocks, toward my favorite beach: Makalawena. I could fly to Umberto's body and tell everybody he is not dead. I could mourn at home or help with the funeral. Instead, I am blissfully driving around in my new car. It feels like the best thing to do. In my mind's eye, I see the letters and names again. Black and white.

I get out of the car, and the sand feels so wonderful and warm under my feet. The ocean is deep blue and surreal like always here. Nowhere the ocean is deeper green, the white sand and coral more white, and the black rocks more black. It always invokes images of long- lost times, of mermaids and water nymphs, pirates, boats, and ship ropes. Yes, old seasoned ship ropes— just like the cord with Umberto.

"Hey, what are you doing here?" I suddenly hear a surprised male voice coming from behind me. I turn around and see his muscled, shiny, brown-bronzed body. Mike has clear blue eyes, white hair, and the broadest smile. Mike became a colleague at the cafe a week ago. He comes fresh from an ice-cold area in the middle of the mainland. He is young and full of life.

"Too bad I have to go." He points at a group of guys that walk in the distance over a narrow white shell path surrounded by the greenest leaves. "I will see you tomorrow again, okay? We should get together someday."

"Yeah, cool!" I say quickly, while I feel a slight blush, and my mind starts spinning. Those eyes looked with more than just interest at my rainbow bikini. I love the attention. "Hey, do you feel like coming by after my morning shift? I live at Kealakekua Bay, down Napoopoo Road, first house on the left. Maybe we could go swim or something."

"Okay, deal," he yells back as he joins the little group.

In the distance, I see him looking back one more time. He sticks his hand up in the air.

I put my hand up a little too enthusiastically and immediately bring it down. *What did I do? How can I be so crazy to invite this guy to my house, especially with Umberto floating around like that?* I try to tell myself that an innocent swim together is not such a big deal.

Pele

"YOU HAVE A date."

I look at the screen where the familiar letters appear again. For six days, he has been floating between heaven and earth. His body is in a coma in Los Angeles. The letters feel so alive. I can almost hear his tone; it is indignant and angry.

"Indeed, but it is nothing," *Why should I apologize?* Umberto sees every move I make while my new life continues.

"Pele the goddess is very real, Christel. Pele is angry. She will destroy. She is dangerous."

I burst out laughing. I am all tangled up with my guilt toward Umberto, and he starts to mention Pele! Pele is the Hawaiian volcano goddess. Pele is the goddess of passion. Every eruption of her volcano in Kilauea on the south of the Big Island is a sign of her passion and her desire to be with her true love. Pele is such a reality for the Hawaiians. There are so many stories about her jealousy, her destruction, and her creation force. Pele is such a reality for me.

"What do you mean?"

"She is angry and wants to express it. There is going to be a new lava eruption at the Kilauea Crater. It will wake up people."

I feel peaceful again in my power. I am on the Big Island, which is where Pele lives. The active Kilauea Crater is very close. I read the other day that they are expecting an eruption again. It is always flowing, sending red-hot lava into the ocean. When it reaches the ocean, it sizzles and makes a gigantic steam plume.

The words continue on my screen: "The Hawaiians give Pele so much power. That is why she is so mighty."

"What do you mean?"

"Because they give her so much power, she gets it. She really exists, Christel. I can see her right now. She is angry, really angry."

"Yes, I know she really exists." In a flash, I am back in that little cave, smelling the sulfur on my first visit to Hawaii. Her voice was so clear and so vivid. She was singing in Hawaiian at first and then said, "There is a place for you." She showed me a picture of a little white house. Six months later, I live in one of the only little white houses on the Big Island. "But why is she angry?"

"She is angry because there is no respect for her. There is no respect for the *aina*, the land. There is too much tension that has to come out. Help. Help! There is fire everywhere! Help. I am in the fire! It is getting so hot; please help me! I am burning!"

I can feel Umberto's fear. My veins quickly fill with fear. The garden around me looks ominous. Scary shadows are moving up and down. I try to sit up and take a deep breath. It is just part of what Umberto is going through. *This must be the second bardo.* I see Jhampa again, telling me about delogs, sticking out his tongue, and pretending to be a frightening demon. Umberto has his own version of it. The Hawaiian version has Pele as the main character, and I am swept away in fear.

I tell myself to concentrate on my breath, glancing at the shadows around me. It is not me in the bardo. I am already too far in it. I hear voices lamenting, voices screaming, and wailing. Louder and louder, penetrating the inside of my ears, the inside of my head and slipping into the crevices in my brain. I glimpse a painting by Hieronymus Bosch, and I am in it, and even more I hear what it sounds like: shrieking sounds of metal and squeaking machines. They are grating in one horrible, destructive sound. I smell blood and tar. Droplets of blood spread around my ears. The hot tongues of fire lick me.

It is so strong and so real. I grab the cushion on the chair and clench my teeth, afraid to be launched into the abyss. Why can't I step out of it? It is not me! I am just experiencing what he is experiencing. It is all an illusion created by his mind. I start panting. The anguish is unbearable. I try to take a deep breath to rise above it, and when I look at my screen, there is no more message. My fingers seem to be frozen. I am not able to type. For the first time, I panic. *Umberto! Umberto! Where are you?* I want to reach him, but I am scared to death that I will be dragged in. This invisible force is so close. It is ready to absorb me and everything I am.

It is just fear that I am feeling. I am not my fear. I try to tell myself. I can make a choice. I can step out of it. "Layka? Where are you, Layka? Please help me, Layka" I am frozen in the chair, and my Kooikerdog is nowhere to be seen.

Minutes pass as I stare at the screen in front of me, and I feel like he is taken away.

"Umberto is in the hole."

My eyes widen. Everything stops. The sounds are gone. A desolate battlefield is all that is left. I see the same handwritten letters in my Yahoo box. *It is talking about Umberto in the third person. I have lost him! Could this be somebody else? Where does this message come from? Who is saying this? Something has taken over.*

"Are you there, Umberto?" My fingers are heavy like cement.

"This is Ferdie. Umberto is in the hole. He will burn and suffer. He is tied down with chains and will be taken over the bridge."

Ferdie? Ferdie? Who is Ferdie? Umberto must be in this state of meeting utter hell, the personifications of his own fear, with all the demons and monsters that Jhampa described in the second bardo. *I know it is just an illusion, but why am I so affected?*

"I murdered my father."

With a smash, I close the top of my laptop and run inside.

"Please help me out of this!" I scream. I know that nobody can hear me. The houses next to me are empty vacation rentals. The family next to me left today. The house shakes for a moment as the door hits the threshold behind me. Panting and shaking, I drop to the floor. I crawl under the coffee table and plug in the lamp.

I hear her nails tapping on the laminate floor. Layka comes running toward me. She is crawling under the table, pushing her wet nose against my face, and curling up against me. She is stretching her paws, and her tail is slapping against the wall. She is licking my face all over. I can feel the same stretching in my body. It feels so good. Every vertebrae crackles, and my power comes back.

"Where *were* you, Layka?"

She acts as if nothing ever happened.

"Oh, Layka. I took myself so seriously!" I laugh and roll with her on the ground.

She jumps on top of me and sneezes with excitement.

I step toward the door, turn the knob, and open the door. A strong flower scent penetrates my nostrils: night-blooming jasmine! My closed laptop, as a locked door to Umberto, is still on the table. For a moment, I hesitate. When I open the laptop, I fill my lungs with air and inhale the scent. I feel strong. The calm rustling of the palm leaves is comforting. The conversation is still on the screen.

New words appear: "You left me. I lost you all of a sudden."

"No. I didn't leave you. Somebody else came between us."

"Somebody else? What do you mean? There was this guy he said he murdered his father. Did you talk to him too?"

"Yes. His name was Ferdie. It was horrible, Umberto. I disconnected. I was afraid—like you. For a moment, I thought it was Lucifer. Where are you now?

You really talked to him?"

"Yes. His name was Ferdie. He said he was going to take me over the bridge. I never went, and now I am in Jayapura. I have no idea how I got here."

"Can you go back to your body?"

"No, I have tried to go back in my body, but I can't. For a while, my heart stopped, but it started beating again. I was hanging above it for a little while; blood came out of my mouth. I am back in Jayapura. It is so weird that I always seem to come back to the garden or to Jayapura where I was born. I love it here. I am so happy that I am out of it. It was hell."

"Yeah, it was horrible. I thought so too, but I realized I could just step out of it when Layka came to save me. I realized how serious I had taken it. I can feel everything you are going through, Umberto. I could even hear it!"

"Hear?"

"Yes. The sharp sound was so threatening, and people were screaming. I was in the middle of it. It was so real."

"That is exactly it: screaming people, clanging metal, and incredible heat. I saw Pele, and that is when we were still connected. She pulled me into that boiling lava with her long hair. Her eyes were spitting fire. There was fire everywhere around me. It was so hot. My whole body was in flames. There were all these people connected to one another with chains. They were screeching horrifically. They tried to pull me down into the abyss and over that bridge."

The horror movie of a few minutes ago is over. I feel incredible relief. I am sure it is similar to the relief that Umberto is experiencing. We seem to be so connected in everything that he is going through. Despite the cord that I cut, I can still feel the emotions with him. It is so strange. His body is still in a coma, but it seems to be such a little part of what he is going through.

I lean back in the chair as it starts to drizzle. The smell of fresh rain enters my nostrils. I repeat the words I wrote in my notebook on the day I returned to the Big Island: "You will be a witness, and it will expand your consciousness way beyond what you ever thought was possible."

I shake my head. I can feel the depth and truth of the words, which I initially felt so much resistance to. Over and over again, I feel the contrast I am to all that pulls him down. I am the light to his heaviness, darkness, and depression. It is not a classic love story. It is not a "they lived happily ever after" or a perfect picture. A messy, deep truth is being revealed before my own eyes: Life doesn't end when we don't see it anymore.

How could I ever tell this at the Sixth Sense Center? They are so "spiritually correct," tame, and conformed, not even a toenail dipped in the ocean of life. Their ten protocols have to be performed before something can happen. They look at the world through a minuscule frame. They have forgotten how blood flows, how pain feels, and how we breathe life. I am the wolf in sheep's clothes, the elephant in the china cabinet. I am moving on forbidden terrain—or terrain that is ignored. I communicate with a dead boyfriend—and I even got to visit him in hell.

The Unfolding

I HAVE CHATTED a few times now with Aran in Los Angeles. Every day, he visits Umberto in the hospital. Yesterday he told me that blood had come out of Umberto's mouth. When I told him I knew that already, he was intrigued about my conversations with Umberto. Up until then, he just knew about it. I was also able to share specific details about the reality of Umberto's body right there where he was: more than 2,500 miles away. I knew that he would be back—no matter how much damage there is in his liver or his kidney, no matter how lifeless he looks on the machines, and no matter how long his heart and lungs have stopped working.

Aran starts to reveal more about Umberto's background. He tells me he is not surprised that this is all happening, especially because of the curse that has been following him since he was nine. When Umberto was young, he was told many times that he would perform miracles one day.

Ever since the cutting of the cord—and since he visited hell—Umberto and I now have a different connection. We are closer in some ways and more detached or neutral in others. We still communicate and are connected, but even more than before, we seem to have our very own version of a connected reality. My words sometimes instantly become a reality on his side—and the other way around.

It is Friday night, and I just got back from work. I'm not really tired, but I'm curious about where Umberto is. The response is immediate as ever. He tells me he is in the garden, feeling separate, disconnected, and lonely.

"Can you feel that you are connected? That you always are connected? That there is a bigger meaning behind it all?" I look at the letters I just typed, but there is no time to reflect.

I hear two long buzzes. My laptop shoots a few centimeters into the air and starts to shake like a broom in a *Harry Potter* movie. Shaking so fast that it almost becomes invisible. I jump up, the chair falling with a loud smack on the ground. Flabbergasted I look to see what is happening. Holding my breath, but it is not fear ... an intriguing curiosity pulls my attention like a magnet. Something starts to accelerate and now it could go in all directions. As if the whole laptop would like to dematerialize. Or fly away, or explode. But with a soft movement it comes down, like it is falling on a feather pillow. It's not exactly what I would expect from a heavy old HP computer. Then it is back here again, as if nothing ever happened ...

A message appears: "Are *you* connected?"

Trembling, I pick up my chair. In a haze, I rub my hands together. I am afraid of getting a shock when I touch the keyboard. I stare at the letters. They look exactly like Umberto's, yet it doesn't feel like him. A strange scent penetrates my nostrils.

Are you connected? Who could that be? Just like Ferdie in hell talked to me before it seems like somebody else, or even more, something took over, like a force or better: an intelligence. My heart is beating in my throat, and the letters are buzzing in my head. But not in a way Umberto would stir in me: if it had come from his mouth, it would have been pedantic—like saying you are connected and you are going to church or you don't and are not connected to God or anything else. These letters sound friendlier, simple, and expansive.

"Are *you* connected?" It appears again.

Warmth gushes up my spine and down my front. My central channel is fully open, as Shen would say, and my mouth instantly fills with saliva. My body seems to have its own response. Every cell in my body fully ignites in bliss. This is it! The image of the floating, vibrating computer is stuck in my mind. Like utter creation force, it could instantly dissolve, transform, or change. I saw it bypassing all physical laws with my own eyes.

"Umberto, did you hear that too? My whole computer started to shake, and there was this loud harsh tone," I type as fast as I can, but there is no answer. It is utterly silent for a while.

It never takes very long before he answers.

I stretch my arms and grab a juicy orange from the bowl. I give it a good bite, just like Umberto would, eating it whole, juice flows all over my chin. I feel the pits touching my teeth as I start to chew.

Pling!

I jump up and throw the rest of the orange to the side.

"Did we speak before?"

What a strange question. I am glad it sounds like Umberto again. "Yes. What do you mean?"

"A loud voice was calling me—an enormous being on a throne. It was God who created the earth and all the beings on it."

I shake my head and burst out laughing. To have Umberto now name it God feels like condensing it in a tiny box: Umberto's box. The experience seems to be so much more expansive than everything I believe to be God. I don't believe in a man on a throne or a woman or something with power that creates victims and suffering. I would call it intelligence, something inside of everything, the omni-creativity, the all-penetrating intelligence, or … the Unfolding. That what made Umberto and me connect in the first place.

Umberto had his own experience, and he calls it God. We both got our very own experience of another realm. He is going through it, and I am the witness. In a flash, I see Jhampa's face again. I hear him saying, "This must be the end of the second bardo, the place of enlightened beings, of gods and goddesses, of that which is beyond duality or even beyond our world, of the crystalline realms, that where everything is beyond form, just pure essence. Umberto had his very own Christian version, and you had yours … just like you experienced your fears in your way, and for Umberto it was hell. Now you experience the divine in your own way."

"I have so much pain in my body. My cancer is almost healed now. I am so hungry. I have such a pain in my neck and shoulders. Where is your date actually?"

My date? You just saw God, you are back in your body, and now you are talking about my date? The date I never had—and maybe never will?

Before I can answer, Umberto already seems to have moved on to another subject. Like so many times now he quickly moves from one state to the other, like all beings without a body.

"Something is going to happen on Kauai … water, a lot of water. Oh, I have so much pain in my body."

Last Check

"WHERE ARE THEY?" Aleida is yelling through the phone when I arrive at the cafe. She is new, she is very capable, and with her dark curls, she looks like a Spanish flamenco dancer. When I enter, she is on the phone. She looks bewildered. It is strange to see her like this. Pearls of sweat run down her neck.

A few days ago, I was fired from my job as a waitress. Tom, the boss had told the other workers at the Aloha Angel Café that I was not really fitting into the team and that I took too much time off to visit Honolulu. I never really felt like a waitress, I never was able to juggle those plates, and the need for filling up the little saltshakers was never something I saw coming. Now I have come to pick up my last check. It feels like a ticket to freedom.

"Where are they?" Aleida yells.

More people enter the hallway, impatiently waiting for coffee. She is the one who brings them to their tables and operates the espresso machine. In front of her is the display of delightful pies, scones, brownies, and cookies. The lilikoi bar is my favorite.

Her tone is now even louder and demanding, panicking. Her eyes are red. A few people walk outside, shaking their heads. She turns around and says,

"Kauai … the dam breached. I don't know where he is!" She throws herself forward and sobs on the showcase. "My son!"

"What is it?" I say and half tripping over the electricity cords on the ground I step towards her and grab her shoulders. Her eyes are red when she looks at me. "Take a deep breath."

She is shaking. She closes her eyes and takes a breath. "My son lives on

150

Kauai with his dad in Kilauea. Because of all the rain, a dam broke and took seven houses into the ocean. They don't know who is missing. I am not able to reach his dad."

Umberto ... water ... Kauai? Now I am here with Aleida crying in my arms. "What shall I do? What shall I do?" she wails.

I turn around and gesture to the people to find themselves a table.

"All right, Aleida. Isn't there another way—"

Aleida pushes through the crowd. "I know, I know!" She sticks up a finger in the air. "I can call my mother who lives close by to see if she can go over there." Nervously, she hits the buttons. Her mother doesn't know anything but will go over there.

Aleida and I sit on a bench in front of the pink building.

"I just went to see him last weekend. He is seven years old and lives with his dad." She tells me about him. Just when she wants to blow her nose again, the phone rings. *Saved!* Just ten minutes before it happened, the two had left the house to look at the surf—way earlier than they usually left the house. On any other day, they still would have been there—and it would have been fatal. Their whole house was gone—taken by the water like a box of matches and brought to the ocean. They lost everything. Aleida cannot help but laugh. All the tension bursts out at once.

"My son is alive! Alive!" she screams at the top of her voice.

The curious customers applaud us. Everybody is cheering now standing around us in a circle. Aleida and me, together in the centre of the attention.

For a moment, I imagine how it would feel to say, "And Umberto is alive too! Even though he is in a coma, he is alive." To tell the whole crowd my story, even that he told me about lots of water in Kauai already yesterday. Tom comes outside and barks, "What is the matter here?"

An old lady outside of the circle appeases him what happened. Without even responding he points at me and says: "You must be here to get your *last* check."

151

Dolphin Heaven

I WAKE UP when I hear a voice. I clearly hear somebody calling my name. It is Adam from two houses down. "Are you coming? The dolphins are there!"

"Okay. I'll be right down!" I call back to him.

"I'll wait for you."

I jump out of bed and search for my best bikini—the orange one with the rainbows on it. When I come downstairs, he is patiently waiting in the lazy chair on the lanai. He has sparkling eyes, a handsome face, big hands, and a chest full of curly black hair.

"And how are you, lady?"

I sigh deeply and look at him suggestively.

"I saw the dolphins jumping this morning." He smiles. "I was sure you would love to join me. It is a beautiful day."

We walk a little way in silence, a scent of flowers passes us. A lot of people have already gathered to gaze at the ocean.

Now and then, I hear an enthusiastic yell as another dolphin playfully shoots out of the water. The spinners are very good at giving a show. The surf looks wild today. It is quite a task to swim through. A few women gracefully dive through the waves; they are there almost every day. A few guys want to follow them, but they have no sense of the rhythm of the waves. The first one is immediately knocked down by a huge wave, and the others are just able to crawl back to the rocks.

"The Big Island is not for pussies," a deep male voice says from behind me as the next wave takes the other two guys into the white swirling foam.

Adam runs toward them and is able to pull the two back on the shore. The third has passed the surf and waves triumphantly back at us.

"He could have been dead," the voice behind me says.

When I turn back, I see a familiar face. He smiles at me as I recognize those eyes: the Hawaiian who pointed out my aumakua: the shark, right here that first day. I smile back at him.

The dolphins are still jumping. I put on my fins and slide into the shallow water. At exactly the right moment, I gracefully push myself through the first wave and swim quickly through the surf. It is all about timing.

When I look up, Adam is swimming next to me. With us there is another group entering the water. A few people just came back and all seem in bliss. "Fantastic" I hear somebody yell with the brightest pink snorkeling gear. At that moment I can see a group of seven dolphins swimming exactly under me. I feel no hesitation and dive toward them. They change course and dive down. I am now right behind them. Faster and faster they move into the depth, and I am in their wake.

Their pace is way too fast for me as a human to keep up with I vaguely realize, but I am already taken into the depth, into their flow. Like a dolphin, I shoot down.

When I bob my head above the water, I realize the only thing I can remember is that incredible speed that took me down. It was effortless. I entered a timeless space, but I couldn't remember it. At some point, I felt an urge to go back up again. I have no idea about time, but there is no sense of being out of breath. I feel extremely light.

"Ten minutes! Ten minutes! You have been down ten minutes!" Adam says when he sees me. "We saw you were taken in this fast movement into the depths. Then something really strange happened. It was as if you disappeared through an invisible glass wall. Your legs were still visible, but your upper body had disappeared … had become invisible. Just like the dolphins all seem to enter another dimension. Going through an invisible wall after which they all disappeared out of sight. I have heard about it from others before, but I never saw it with my own eyes."

An older, bald man with a penetrating liquid blue gaze looks at me. He is amazed and worried at the same time. He looks like an experienced swimmer. Next to him are two women, clearly very impressed. They cannot really believe what they saw.

"I have heard about people entering another dimension for a long time," Adam says, "but I never thought I would see it with my own eyes."

Every memory is erased from my brain. The only thing that remains is a fleeting sense of flying underwater. The dolphins were flying with me—through an extremely bright sky and with incredible speed.

I feel the desire to feel solid ground under my feet. In the distance, I see little creatures on the shore. I notice how tired my body is. I am glad we swim back in a group.

I sigh deeply and lay myself on the warm lava rocks. I close my eyes, and my whole body trembles. My cells are sparkling. It seems like my body is still spinning at high speed. Swimming with the dolphins always makes me slightly nauseous in a way I actually enjoy. The sun burns on my skin.

When I sit up, the dolphins are out of sight. The cars at the bay have disappeared. No waves, no swimmers.

"Are you coming?" Adam stretches out his hand to help me up.

"Yes, I got so hungry."

***

When I get home, there is a text message from Los Angeles on my computer. "Urgent," it says. I am reluctant to read it. I am still so full of the dolphins.

"Hello, Christel. This is Aran. Call us as soon as possible. Umberto just woke up. His heart stopped for a while, and he just woke up. He keeps on saying he wants to speak to you. We are trying to reach you."

I feel my heart sink, but still I pick up the phone and call Umberto. "You were dead again? You are declared dead again?" I am surprised by my tone. Sweat drips down my belly from the hot sun. I see traces of white salt on my legs like little islands.

He confirms that it happened an hour ago, and his words vibrate in my head like a giant bell. It happened an hour ago—*right when I was diving down with the dolphins.*

For the very first time, I am not impressed by his return from death. For the first time, I feel rather irritated. I don't want to hear about his dying, death certificates, or his family dealing with the hospital. Ever since the cutting of the cord, I don't want to be confronted by a distant body that is dying. Umberto playing with life or life playing with him or his not choosing. More then ever before, I want to move on with my life. It starts to dawn on me how much our lives are connected.

I don't want to hear the amazingly good things that happen to Umberto on the other side: angels drinking out of golden teacups in a land without shadow, eternal dogs always happy in big fields freed forever from their illnesses, loving guides that bring him to special places, show him secrets, and have plans for him, angels four times as big as humans with four wings on their backs, flowers and buildings and colors, so beautiful, so wonderful, and exotic, so beyond imagination and limitless that it might even be boring, gods on thrones with fingers moving, granting begging babies their wish to be born, stairs going so high in heaven that the light is impossible to withstand so you have to eat a certain brown gooey stuff to continue, or lovemaking so naked, so endless, so dripping, so exciting, so deep and luscious, big and eternal, that everybody is doing it, up, under, over, with each other and alone, dramatic, poetic, and pensive. On the other hand, there is the darkness, where fear reigns—where they are still screaming and burning and feeling bad and mean and desperate in hell, in the fire, over the bridge.

I don't want to hear it anymore. After all, it is just his expression. But how much are we really connected?

I believe we all know about these other realms. We don't need another eyewitness like me. We have all been there in some way—long before or right before we were born. Why does the illusion seem so real? Why does it feel so real to sit on this side of the window and know all this, feel all this, smell all this, and feel it so close through him, so present so alive, but still we go back to our cars, to the road to nowhere, to our homes, to our jobs, and to the ones we think are our lovers. We do it all. We change our brakes, put new fluid in, listen to what the others say and go back to that miniature life that sometimes feels like a prison. We listen to what doctors say and what machines tell us, and we believe what we are told about the world.

The Date

WITH MY EYES closed, I turn the faucet for a little more hot water. I get chicken skin. My arms firmly push against my body, my head is down, and I rock slowly. Now it all comes back. Here in the outside shower, behind the house, under the traveler's palm: the stepping out of his body and the immediate longing for my body that followed. That was seven months ago. He has been in Los Angeles for two months.

This morning, I got a message from his aunt in Los Angeles. They were so excited yesterday when he woke up from death. I got to talk to him briefly, and it was so unexpected when he slipped into a coma again today. I am almost immune to the fact that he is in a deep coma. Alive or not, it seems impossible to digest. The letters on my screen are undeniable. I have been saving our conversations on my computer for a while.

Ever since his words appeared in the Yahoo box, his texts prove themselves true. Just like with delogs, it is as if the physical state of his body is subordinate to what is really happening—to what I get to witness.

Just for one short moment, I imagine his beautiful, strong body against mine. With my eyes closed, I turn up the heat a little. Again, more chicken skin. Is he really with me again? Is it wishful thinking?

"Hello!" I hear Mike's voice next to me.

I shriek and pull my towel around my body. The hot water is still running. I feel a little gawky and know he has seen me naked in the shower—with my sensual thoughts. "Mike? What are you doing here?"

"I know that you don't work at the cafe anymore, and I thought I'd see where she is. I also felt like a jump in the water." He looks at me from head to toe, showing his wide smile.

I chuckle back.

"What a surprise … what a nice surprise."

"How are you?"

"Good, very good." The words come out of my mouth a little too fast. My thoughts are racing. *Umberto's life is hanging on a thread. Umberto just survived hell, saw God, had blood coming out of his mouth, and is in a coma again. He can see everything. I don't want him to see everything. Nee, Potverdorie! He needs to mind his own business.*

Mike is staring at the Jacuzzi.

"You feel like going in?"

"Yes." He pulls of his shirt, puts his feet in first, and slides into the warm water.

I hesitate. I am still naked under that wet towel. "Wait. Let me get my bathing suit."

He chuckles approvingly. Inside the house, the panic rushes through my head. *Umberto … dead, what to do? I cannot … now … help.* In a hurry, I pull up my bathing suit, sweating and jumping around.

"Wow. What a great spot you have here." Mike watches me slide into the hot water.

My panic fades. The thought about Umberto disappears to the background. I sigh and feel relaxed in the warm bubbling water.

"Great." Mike nods encouragingly when he sees me relax.

I start to feel comfortable with this beautiful young body. I take a deep sigh and realize the absurdity of it all. Umberto is floating between heaven and earth. I do not know if he is really coming back. He was jealous about Mike a few days ago. Now I actually have that notorious date he was talking about. *How would he be? Will he still be able to choose? What is left from standing up against a tsunami like he did the first time? Would he be able to see me right now?*

I look at the beautiful young god in my Jacuzzi, smile, and shake my head.

"What is the matter?" Mike asks.

"Nothing." I turn myself toward him, and my leg touches his under the water. I sigh deeply. The attraction between us is inevitable. I am surprised that I don't feel guilty. It just is what it is. Umberto is sort of dead, and I am here with Mike in the Jacuzzi.

"Life is beautiful," he says with his husky, sultry voice. "Such a beautiful clear day." He takes a long pause while looking up at the azure sky. "You look beautiful."

I close my eyes. It feels like such a precious moment. When I open my eyes, I feel the urge to kiss him. Instead, I keep a respectful distance.

Then the phone rings.

"Saved by the phone." Mike laughs as I hurry inside, glad to be distracted.

"Strange. Usually I only have reception outside the house."

Unknown number. Who could that be? It is almost one thirty. I pick up. Nothing—and then a weird noise like from underwater, a strange buzz. It sounds vaguely like voices.

"Hello? Hello? Who is there?"

I hear a strange sound and something like voices in the background. It is very deep and vague, rustling like an echo. A voice says, "Me ... it is ... me ..."

"Umberto? Is that you?" I hold the little phone away from me and look at it. I cannot believe I just heard his voice. "Where are you, Umberto?" I yell in the phone. I peek through the little window.

Mike just moves his big hand through his hair with a big smile. His arms are shiny in the sun. I sigh forcefully and press the little phone against my ear. Nothing ... only rustling.

Again, I look at Mike. "I am just going to the other side of the street ... better reception there!" I'm happy that I have an excuse. "Umberto?"

His voice is suddenly clear. "I am here. My body is in a coma. Christel, there are so many voices. I am going to a school ... the copper school." It feels like so much is happening around him.

"Umberto, you are calling me *on the phone! On the phone!*"

"What?"

"You are calling me on the phone ... with your almost-dead body!"

"Yes, I can hear your voice too," he answers.

I reach the edge of the ocean and sit down. The flowers smell wonderful. It seems like I am smelling another flower. The scent again seems to fade, and it is subtler. I can smell the place where Umberto is. It is sweet and strong. I hear more rustling. I push my phone against my ear and want to crawl through it to his side.

"I have to go. They are calling. I am going to the copper school."

"I love you," I say, but Umberto has hung up.

Bewildered I look at the little screen: "End of conversation with unknown number." I see it for another second, and then it is gone. I just called heaven—or was it not heaven? What did he say again? He is in the copper school? And his body is in a coma in Los Angeles. Why did he call me? Did he see me sitting in the Jacuzzi? He didn't seem to be particularly jealous.

Lost in thoughts, I slowly walk home. A red truck passes by. I look up, and somebody waves at me vigorously. It is Richard. I haven't seen him for a while. I close up like a clam. My experience—so vulnerable, so palpable—lingers. Richard is the last person I could ever tell. Richard, my first landlord when I just moved to the Big Island, offered me a tiny white house in exchange for watering his gardens.

"Hey, how are you?" he yells. "You look good." He looks me over from head to toe with his brown, virile eyes that always seem a little too greedy.

I feel slightly uncomfortable. I take a deep breath, and it just comes out of me. "Do you remember that guy who came back from death? Believe it or not, he died again. He's actually in a coma right now, and he just called me from heaven." I feel relieved. It just came out of me. I didn't even care how. "Now … just a minute ago." I point at the little phone in my hand.

Richard looks at me for a moment with bewildered eyes. Then he starts laughing. A deep laugh merging into a roar, his car slightly shaking.

I cannot but laugh with him. It is too crazy to make up. Just because it is so absurd, it feels so good to just laugh with Richard about it: Richard, who is only interested in food and women. I feel no disapproval, nothing.

I lean forward again with laughter and feel like I am totally losing it, another car approaches from the other side.

"I have to go," he yells. In his mirror, I can see his laughing continue, shaking his head.

When I turn around, Mike appears from behind the house. He is wearing his blue shorts and white shirt again, his hair is still wet.

"Where were you?"

"I was just coming back."

"You have been gone for more than an hour." I hear the disappointment in his voice.

"More than an hour?"

"Yes, it is two thirty, I have to go. I have to work at four."

"Sorry that it took me so long." I am desperately looking for the reason why it took so long. At most, I talked to Umberto for five minutes. Where did the time go?

"It doesn't matter, I invited myself in the first place."

He gives me a big hug, and we hold each other for a long while. In the embrace, I feel my confusion settle.

He steps into his little blue Toyota, radiant as ever. I stare at him driving away, and my mind is already back at that strange conversation. It really felt like five minutes. There are still fifty-five mysterious missing minutes remaining—like it has happened so many times when Umberto is wandering around. Time seems to be nonexistent, stretched out, or missing—just like in my one breath down with the dolphins.

I sigh. In a way, I am happy that nothing happened between Mike and me.

The Curse

IT IS NOVEMBER 2006. Umberto has finally woken up and returned from Los Angeles. For the very first time, he will come to me: to the Big Island, to my island, to my life. There had always been an ocean between us, a forty-five-minute flight, or three thousand miles between us when he was in Los Angeles. That distance somehow gave enough space for our communications to take place.

I didn't feel the urge to visit him in Los Angeles, and I didn't have the money. It seemed like engaging with the reality of his body would take away from the experience of our communications. Each time Umberto entered his body again, my voice would fade away, he couldn't hear me anymore. It was impossible to connect. And much more than the distance, there had been something else in the way: the curse.

He had hardly talked to me about it from the other side, but Umberto would report about it after he was back alive. The forty-one spirits were after him, and he had to fight them every time he entered a coma. Each time, he said he conquered a few more. It sounded so unreal to me; I could never really wrap my thoughts around it. It always made me slightly irritated, and it made me think about the dark cloud I saw next to his head flittering like a bat when we were together. It became real when he was communicating to me from the coma in Los Angeles.

***

A big black moth is flying against the window of my bedroom. Now and then, it disappears behind the curtains. It is the only window that doesn't open.

Layka starts to bark, barking in a void it seems like. She is looking at the butterfly. I sit on the bed with my computer on my lap. I am chilly and am just about to get up to find a shawl. She is only three feet away, and her barking gets louder. Her body squirms. Foam appears around her bare teeth. The butterfly above her flutters vigorously to escape. It looks like invisible forces are trying to catch it. I know this barking. I know it really well.

Kooikerdogs don't bark, it is not in their make- up. Only if there is a really good reason they bark. In my acupuncture practice, she would sometimes stare and bark at people, until they felt something leave. And now she does it again. Right now, when Umberto is floating again between two worlds, again in another coma.

I stand up and resolutely take the big butterfly in between my hands, and open the door with my elbow. For a moment, I just stand there and open my hands. It stops fluttering, and sits there for a moment. As if catching its breath from all the effort it just went through. Opening and closing its wings gently, no more trace of her struggle. I admire the carefully laced pattern. "What was happening to you, big butterfly? Why were you struggling?"

It sits there without moving, then it flies away, quickly disappearing in the dark night.

Layka starts to wag her tail.

I sit back on my bed and stare at the computer screen in front of me.

"Thank you, Christel. They don't want me to do the ceremony. That is why they want to keep me captured. You just saved me from those spirits."

"What? You mean that butterfly was you? And I saved you by letting you go outside?"

"Yes. That was me."

I have seen the black butterfly so many times, and I made the connection with Umberto. More and more, it had become undeniable.

Google says, "In Hawaii, if a loved one has just died, the moth is an embodiment of the person's soul returning to say good-bye." It seems unmistakable. He somehow has to end the influence of the forty-one spirits to not have to die again, and for that, he needs to come to the Big Island.

***

162

When I get to hear it out of the mouth of Aunty Moana, it becomes more real. For the very first time, I get to talk to her on the phone. Her voice sounds broad and grounded and full of life. It is the opposite of Umberto's mumbling. I imagine a big, powerful Hawaiian woman. It is a delight to listen to her. She knows about the conversations between Umberto and me. On Friday, they will come to the Big Island to do a Ho'oponopono ceremony. It literally means "to set things right" in Hawaiian.

"Our ancestors were in really powerful positions—from an Ali'i ancestry. There is so much mana in the family, but they have misused their power in the past. They broke a lot of kapu laws—the laws that put the Ali'i on the commoners— and they killed many innocent people. It all came back to Umberto. His mother knew it when he was born. She knew it would come back to her through him. When he was old enough, they did the ceremony—but it turned out to be a curse. Every time he came to the Big Island, he got sick or had really bad luck. Thanks to all the mana that the family had acquired, he was able to rise above the laws of nature and perform incredible miracles. But it is just not right," Aunty Moana says. To hear it from her comforts me. The utterly strange journey Umberto is taking has a source: the curse.

She continues about his body: "He is recovering so fast. It is incredible. The doctors cannot believe it. Oh, we have so much to tell you. Those guys in the hospital are crazy. They just want to deny everything that happened. We even had to sign a paper that we won't disclose anything. Anyway, he is back now. I am so glad that I was able to trace the name of the head of the spirits that Umberto gave me. Henikala was a chief on the Hilo side, next to the volcano."

Ceremony

UMBERTO IS ON the Big Island for the first time since we met. He is only a two-and-a-half-hour car ride away in Hilo. I cannot go see him. I am in the middle of a retreat with Han and Betty. They are my guests from Holland for five more days, and it is impossible to leave them for Umberto's ceremony. In an hour, it will happen. He calls me when I arrive with Han and Betty in Honaunau at the city of refuge.

Umberto's voice trembles on the phone. "An hour ago, we arrived in Pahoa. I can see the smoke of the active volcano in the distance, and I can smell the sulfur. Yesterday, we landed late in Hilo."

He says he hasn't slept all night. The yelling, the shadows, and the threat are more intense with every passing hour. Faces that he unwillingly got to know on his travels to the other side. They became so real to me during our lovemaking when we were still together. Brutal, resolute, and demanding, each one confronts him with another fiber of the burden his ancestors passed on to him.

Every time, he hears his name: Henikala, the chief of the group of warriors. A truth he doesn't even fully know or understand, only the unbearable weight of it. The spirits seem to know more then anything their mission: to let him pay the price, to kill Umberto. They are so many, like a web spun around him. They always come at night, he tells me, disappearing at dawn, and he is left feeling tortured, lost, and torn apart.

"No need to fear," the kahuna kept on telling him today.

"But I don't trust it, Christel. I am afraid. I am so afraid."

The Ho'oponopono ceremony did not go well.

At six o'clock, I get a phone call from his aunt. They were on their way to visit me on the sunny side of the island.

During the ceremony, Umberto collapsed and woke up again. He kept complaining about a pain in his side, but nobody paid attention to it. The closer they came, the stronger it got. It was an acute gallbladder attack. Umberto kept describing how the spirits hadn't left during the ceremony. Instead, they put a knife in his liver. When he was brought to the hospital, they operated on him immediately. The sword Umberto had seen now became the knife of the surgeon; it cut straight through his gallbladder and aorta. The surgeon had never something like it happen in his thirty-year career. Umberto has to be airlifted to Honolulu.

The hospital is only a seven-minute drive away from where I live. In a rush, my wet bathing suit still under my dress, I race up the hill to see a little piece of Umberto. A black butterfly flutters in front of my window when I leave. Rain pours down when I reach the top of the hill. *What would I see? How would I respond to his unconscious body?*

He is in my life, in my town, and on my island? I hear the sirens from a distance and see the red lights blinking, the red and white colors of the ambulance in front of me turning onto Mamalahoa Highway, the road I got to know so well. I feel it printed forever on my retina.

Right there behind that closed door is Umberto. It is the closest I've ever been to his collapsed body. I drive behind the ambulance on the way to the airport. When I call his aunt on my cell phone she confirms they just left the hospital with the ambulance. I hit the brake, slow my pace and park right next to the highway. *How ridiculous it is to follow the ambulance, to follow the mayhem, to follow that which hadn't been even a close reality for me before, to follow Umberto's broken body.*

If there is one thing I learned at the Sixth Sense Center, it is the setting of energy. The sense of choice in that what we experience. Keeping focused on the intention underneath it, or even more the knowing that we *are* a spirit and *have* a body. Not wanting to escape the body but rather experience the full self in the body, experience it with all my senses. During all my encounters with Umberto, I kept that belief, and with that I was holding the space for all the unusual experiences, the "out of the box-ness." But now, seeing the shiny ambulance moving away in the rain, the doors with the two windows, the bright lights in it, the red lights blasting urgency, it is all sucked out of me. The high-pitched sound of sirens cuts through my skin, enters my tissue, and creates holes in that which always felt safe. That in which I had *another* connection to Umberto, that which I could always trust, I feel it all seep away. I burst out crying, my arms slumped over the wheel.

I see a tsunami of fights, pain, and desperation that is always so present around Umberto. The weight of his ancestors on his shoulders is presented as real to me. There is no escaping it. I feel the doors closing in on me. His darkness as the rain cloud above us. I see car, after, car after car passing me as if they are all following him and his distress. I want to scream, but I feel so hollow. It is as if I do not exist. The reality is that Umberto's body is moving away from me. The sirens have gone, but the feeling of emptiness stays.

It was his gallbladder this time. In Chinese medicine, the gallbladder represents courage and the ability to cut through and move on to another phase. The image of the ambulance doors is still pulsing in my eyes, and our realities are touching, but all the magic has vanished. Disbelief remains—disbelief that he can ever recover from the cut in his aorta and his gallbladder.

My courage left with his, and I cannot even believe it all ever happened. That which I knew all the way through and always had avoided: to be confronted with the physical state of his body would mean the end of it; would make it impossible to communicate with him the way we did, now proves to be true: it takes it all away. Seeing the reality of his body makes it just like all the other bodies in pain that need to be repaired by doctors, I cannot seem to reach anymore the awareness of his spirit wandering around like a delog. Who am I to think that it could ever be another way than medical science tells us? The doubt is a solid heavy rock pulling me down with more gravity than I have ever felt.

I think about Han and Betty, my retreat guests, anxiously waiting for me on the bottom of the hill, who do not want to hear about this heavy rock. They are eager to hear about my experiences, and I had told them a little bit yesterday. Their eyes brightened, excited to hear more, and they validated somehow that what happened with Umberto is possible. As if a deep buried truth, they always had felt in them had now surfaced: that anything is possible.

Now, in the face of utter disaster, I lost it. At the Sixth Sense Center, they talk about the web of denial that envelops us all. The denial that there is more than we currently see. The denial that we are spirit and have a body. Looking at the ambulance makes me almost forget about delogs. I want to deny that I still believe that he can cure miraculously and that he can talk to me on my computer screen!

I sigh deeply and slowly feel my body relax. I rub my legs with both hands, the touch brings me into my body. It is easy to follow the train of thoughts of what we believe about each other. The fear creates the boundaries of what is possible.

It all flashes by in my mind: the undeniable moments that Umberto's reality merged with mine, the shower where it first happened, the cutting of the cord and his reaction, him talking about what happened to me at the Sixth Sense Center, the keys floating in the air, the scents, the butterfly, his picture on a random screen in Holland, the picture of Karen, my computer jumping up in the air, his predictions like the one about the water in Kauai, and the letters on my screen. I still believe there is another reality beyond this heaviness—beyond what we see. Deep down, I know he is taking another peek on the other side. I take another deep breath and look out over the ocean. The vastness of the water and the blue, pink, and orange hues lift me up.

His body will be lifted soon. The orange sun is almost touching the horizon. In my mirror, I see the dark cloud behind me. Han and Betty probably never had rain back down at the bay.

I feel a lick on my neck. Layka pushes her two front paws against my shoulder. Letting out a little cry, I turn around and gesture her to jump in my lap. The sight of my ever-loyal sweet dog curling up against me softens me more. Tears well up inside me.

I start the car, turn around, and descend slowly, curling back down green Napoopoo Road, back into the last sunlight. I feel my body breathing again. Every curve in the road returns a little more of me with every changing color in the sky. When I finally arrive at the ocean, the sun has set.

Umberto's body will again be a plane ride away. When I set foot on ground in my yard, something has profoundly changed.

Root

WHEN IT RAINS in Hawaii, it pours. When something shifts everything shifts. Something did profoundly shift on November 19, 2006, which happens to be Umberto's birthday. The ceremony had done its job in its own way—for both of us. My retreat guests have left, Umberto has healed miraculously, and he is back in Honolulu. My time on the Big Island will come to an end just as unexpectedly as it came into existence.

Right at this moment under the mango tree, my bare feet on the soft grass, I feel it all come together: the shift I had felt a few days earlier after seeing Umberto in the ambulance, the whisper this morning that told me to move to Kauai, the most northern of the Hawaiian islands, the sudden urge today to go for a short trip to Holland. And now Steve and Louise— the owners of the house I am housesitting—walk into my yard with their news. "The house finally sold, and you have to move out."

It couldn't have been more perfectly orchestrated.

***

Tomorrow, I go to Holland for three weeks. I am sitting at my favorite coral beach in Honaunau for the last time, the place where the whisper had told me all that was about to happen between Umberto and me. I stare at the calm water, which is like a perfect mirror in front of me. I ponder my move to Kauai when I get back to Hawaii. The whisper said, "You are moving to Kauai." It somehow all makes sense. I finally quit the Sixth Sense Centre, the house is being sold and I am moving away from the place of Umberto's curse. It makes me feel like I am moving away from him and all we had. Like it all has ended.

Then my attention shifts. A slight ripple appears on the water, and to my surprise I see my oma appear: my mother's mother. Right above the water. I realize it will be her hundredth birthday in January. She has had Alzheimer's for many years, but her body is as healthy as ever. I haven't seen her in a long time. She is staying in a nursing home and doesn't recognize her seven children anymore. I can clearly see her face in front of me. It makes me close my eyes. I say hello to her like I did so many times to Umberto. I see her in the mist.

Like in a vacuum, I have difficulties reaching her. There is so much confusion around her; somehow it is keeping her stuck where she is. It makes me think of Umberto and his confusion. That must be her dementia. Out of the blue, she starts to talk to me. She is surprised to see me, surprised and not surprised. I can hear her words clearly in my mind: "I don't want it anymore, Christel. I am stuck here. I have been in this for so long."

She tells me how everybody is preparing for her hundredth birthday. Everybody is so excited, and she knows it all: the photo books they are making, the songs, the sketches, the cake, and the speech. "I know everything, although they are all hiding it from me. They all think I am in my childish Alzheimer's brain, but I can see it all, Christel. I don't want to have a celebration. It is all a waste of money."

I open my eyes for a moment and see another ripple on the water. It is like a slight breeze. I close my eyes again. My oma is still clearly in my mind's eye.

"You can choose, Oma. You can choose to step out of it. It is only one step you have to make." I speak aloud. Like I have told Umberto the same thing so many times.

And at that moment I see oma take a step, out of the confusion— the confusion that held her back for decades, a step out of the mist, the isolation, and her sickness. She steps out of this prison and out of the mind she lost. Her face starts to shine and smile, filled with relief. I see her disappear into the light. I open my eyes again. I blink because of the brightness of the reflection of the sun. It all feels so real. My eyes start to tear. I can feel her being lifted up, and I feel the liberation in me. I know, in every fiber of my being, she has chosen.

169

Early the next morning, I get the phone call from mama: Oma has died in her sleep.

***

From the train, I see the flat pastures, the canals in between the windmills, bare winter trees, little houses, and the sunny landscape like a postcard slowly passing by. Dressed in a gray wool vest, a charming long coat, shiny black boots, and matching shawl, my sister is sitting across from me. I can feel Erika's world around her: the physical therapy business she owns, the numbers, the insurances, the ailments of the many clients, the schedules, constrained appointments, the therapy, the classes that she gives. I see the mechanical solutions for the illnesses and the money that flows with it. The five years we are apart feel like a lifetime of differences that cannot be bridged. The firm grasp she has on material reality accentuates the fluidity of my own reality. The train is rocking us forward on our way to the funeral.

I sigh. I do not feel in tune with Holland yet. I look down at my brown velvet pants, the only warm ones I have. My body doesn't want to adapt yet. It wants to be bare, naked, or loosely covered. The Hawaiian air is still around me, and the warmth oozes out of my pores. It is always hard for me to adapt to Holland when I return. After a few days, I realize I don't want to adapt to it. I don't want to adapt to the black and gray clothes everyone is wearing and to the seriousness, the grayness, covering up all the nakedness, making it uniform. I still feel the lush tropical flowers around me and the soft blue water on my body. Even the dolphins are still clicking in my ears.

"Tea?" my sister asks, taking me out of my thoughts. She is always prepared for everything.

"Yes, please," I look at her face as she carefully fills the little ceramic cup she brought for me, her little sister.

We haven't spoken a word yet about the death of Oma.

"You know, Erika, I booked my ticket to Holland two weeks ago. It was so strange. I just knew I *had* to go to Holland right then."

Erika looks at me in a strange gaze.

"What do you mean? You were not going to be there for her hundredth birthday?" she says sternly as if saying: how for god's sake dare you not be there.

"Yes, it was the strangest thing." I pause for a moment. "I always feel when it is the right time to go to Holland—even though it doesn't make sense." I tell her the whole story about Oma and her step forward in the sea.

"What do you mean she was *talking* to you?" Sarcasm appears in my sister's voice.

"You know what I mean … *telepathically*," I say.

"That is what mama told me … that when she called you, you already knew. She couldn't believe it, and I couldn't believe it either," Erika whispers.

I can feel the resistance in her voice. I see the fine lines of her profile reflected in the window. She pushes her lips together and squeezes her eyes. My words stretched her too far. For a moment, I feel the desire to shake her up and scream, "It really happened!"

I have not told her about the experiences with Umberto. She must have heard about it from my parents. I never sensed an ounce of curiosity from her.

The rest of the train ride continues in silence.

***

From where we stand, the illusion seems so real—the illusion of the ultimate end of a life, so definite, the last breath taken, everything cold and stiff, ready to disintegrate as we stand around Oma's body in a beautiful blue dress. Her children are sobbing around her. Her youngest daughter Corina is touching her forehead. It is so real that we cannot even fully imagine the truth. Umberto showed me the truth so many times; there is no real division between life and death.

The whole funeral replays in my mind as I sit in the back of my father's Mercedes on the way home. We dropped off my sister on the train to Germany. I muse about Oma's grandchildren: the swimming champion Joyce, the world famous soccer player Earnie, the screenwriter Dennis, the moviemaker, the children's book writer Jorgen, my niece in Paris flying her own airplane. They all grew up to become strong, positive, and honest humans. They radiate with love for Oma. For a moment, I feel like I am floating in a void. I want to give up living in Hawaii and crawl back into my childhood—or crawl into a safe and ordinary life. I can be like one of them.

Thoughts keep racing through my mind. *Why did I do this again? Why do I live so far away? Why did I have to move so far away from everything that feels familiar and welcoming? Why am I the one who lives on the other side of the world? The place where it is night when it is day here? Why do I have to take that long journey again? Leave everything behind?*

The green pastures are not like friendly distant memories anymore. They demand me to stay. The cows, the windmills, the trees, and the clouds in the sky beg me to take my place between them. Pulling tears out of my eyes. Never before have I felt such nostalgia, such homesickness, such a strange longing to come back

I wonder if I am fleeting into Oma's experience, if I feel what she is feeling, the layers she is going through, the renewed sense of who she is, and what she is leaving behind. As I look at the clouds, I see a face appear. It is my oma. No, it is not my oma. Her face is darker. I can see the eyes. The eyes are so white. It is the blind woman from the lecture on the Big Island! Her words come clearly back in my mind: "Go for it!" She looks me straight in the eye and says, "You think I have been sleeping, but I have been watching you. You have a mission. Go for it!" The words sound half Hawaiian and half English.

On the Dutch pastures, the black and white cows are changing color. A big group of white seagulls flies up into the sky, and I feel a warm glow. "Thank you, kahuna," I whisper.

My whole experience with Umberto—all the wisdom and all the extraordinariness that came out of it—has everything to do with the mission she told me I had. I know now. I am not done with it yet. I look at of my parents in the front of the car. They always look so much smaller than me. My sweet parents are always there for me. They always support my decisions—even the ones beyond their comprehension.

Nothing will explain my irrational move to another island, but I have to go. As soon as I get back to Hawaii, I will move to Kauai, the most northwestern of the Hawaiian Islands. It is the most beautiful of all the islands and has the clearest skies. They call it "the island of plenty." I have no clue what I will be doing there, but I am ready.

Part 3

The Approach

IT IS AUGUST 2007, and after two years, I am back from Kauai in Honolulu for a short visit. I am back in the park where Umberto and I walked so many times. I am on Oahu to get Layka inseminated with Kooiker semen by a female veterinarian on the North Shore. It all started with the fig tree in my new lover Chuck's yard in Princeville on Kauai.

The fig tree is my favorite tree in Chuck's backyard: the bold shape of their leaves as young, determined creative hands stick out in all directions. The few almost-ripe figs sprout triumphantly out of the branches, reaching a deep purple color and soft velvet skin while spreading a lovely smell.

Layka has her favorite spot under the shady tree. A few weeks ago, a beautiful Hawaiian man appeared out of the blue. Without any introduction, he pointed at Layka and said, "Watch out with that dog under that tree. The fig tree symbolizes conscious conception. Female dogs usually get pregnant very unconsciously, but your dog might as well choose to become pregnant." He laughed and disappeared as quickly as he had appeared behind the thick leaves of the shrubs, leaving me with this strange information. I couldn't let go of his words.

A couple weeks later, it all came together. Layka was in heat, and I asked her telepathically if she wanted to get pregnant over and over again. In many subtle ways, she gave me the nudge. It all unfolded within a few days: Kooiker semen from Texas, a veterinarian on Oahu, and a place to stay in Honolulu.

I will be here for two weeks. I couldn't wait to show Layka all the places I started to love so much in the short time I lived here: Diamond Head, Kapiolani Park, Sans Souci Beach, Manoa Valley, and Ala Moana Park. I am walking the same paths with her instead of Umberto, bringing back the memories of our affair. It is as if his footsteps are replaced with Layka's happy paw prints with each step.

I decide to take off my slippers to cross a grassy field in the familiar Ala Moana Park, which is just outside of Waikiki. Layka walks next to me on the leash. The warm grass feels good between my toes. I see a silhouette on the other side of the field. A cement path is filled with joggers, skaters, and bikers. I keep expecting the figure to turn back on the path and vanish or reveal itself as a fragment of my imagination. It comes closer, the dark speck takes shape. I can make out its legs and shoulders. His dark t-shirt and black pants: *Umberto? No ... here? Now?*

The last time we spoke on the phone was about nine months ago. He told me he had moved back to Jayapura. His body had completely returned to health. He didn't feel bothered by spirits anymore, and he had a new girlfriend through the church he had gotten so involved with. We were staying out of each other's lives. It had happened after the ceremony, the gallbladder attack, and the shimmering white doors of the ambulance.

Since my move to Kauai, I felt farther away from everything that had come to pass between us. My life was full of retreats, learning how to surf, and a new lover. I met Chuck the day I arrived on Kauai. The incredible experience with Umberto remained somewhere deep inside my gut, waiting to be digested. Now, I just wanted to take full breaths with a new life.

Layka is on her leash. Her shiny white red fur flutters in the wind, and her tail is proud like a flag. Layka is a symbol of the soon-to-be new life in her belly: the semen from Texas, frozen at the veterinarian in Kailua, ready to be inserted at the right moment.

To my surprise, Layka sees the figure too. An unusual curiosity makes her pull the leash, wanting to go forward. Her focus is on the figure in front of us—not sniffing the grass anymore. We cross the green field, and he is coming straight at us.

This is the first time Layka has seen Umberto in real life. *What is he doing here? Shall I yell? Shall I call his name? I am still too far. Run?* Blood starts pumping in my ears.

Umberto, the one who once was so close, is creating an unfamiliar threat. It is a mistake to meet him here in his body. Layka sneezes like she does when she is excited. Her wet nose sticks forward as if she recognizes him. My feet carry more weight than before, and I am unable to change direction.

The memory of the gray shark flashes through my mind. In my feet, I feel the weight of the denial, the doubt, and Umberto's not choosing all those times. The approach seems like slow motion. The noises of other people have faded. I am walking straight into my past. I hold my breath. I am not imagining this. I am approaching Umberto, and Layka sees it too. *What will I say to him? What will I ask? Why do I feel so nervous? Why does he so feel like a stranger?*

Twenty yards away, his eyes focus on me, but we haven't acknowledged each other yet. I feel a bump in my belly. For a second, I feel my dantian turn. I turn my body to the right and step in a new direction. It is like I am watching myself. The heaviness of my feet seeps away. *Why don't I want to be confronted by him? Why does my body respond this way? Why do I make this turn? It actually feels wonderful, but why?* I walk away from him; every step is a liberation.

My feet are lighter, faster, and stronger. Ten feet, twenty feet, thirty feet. I don't want to look back. I finally stop, turn around, and look straight into the bright sun. Layka is looking behind us. I look up again, expecting to see him really close, but he is gone! Umberto has vanished! *Did he hide? Did he run away? Was it all an illusion?*

I look in all directions. The path along the field still has the same stream of joggers, bikers, and hikers. The field in front of me is empty. I shake my head. Am I crazy? I am so sure that it was him coming here right at me, fully alive. Again I look around me, for a moment I look up, if he maybe has risen up. But I only see the clear sky.

I left my phone in my rental car. My fingers tremble when I call him. I had expected him to be in West Papua.

"… this number is no longer in service," a woman's voice says. We are disconnected, only the powerful surge of my dantian in my belly remains.

The next day, Layka and I return to Kauai. Layka does not get pregnant. The vet tells me at the last moment that she wants to operate on Layka—, cut her open instead of a simple insemination. "Because of the high success rate."

At her test the next day, all Layka's hormone levels collapse. Layka has chosen.

Father

"ALL SOULS?" KATIE tilts her head at me. I am on the most western point of Kauai. It is January 2011, and for the last two nights of the retreat, the three of us will camp on the beach at Polihale.

"Yes, all souls," I answer. "The Hawaiians believe that all souls leave the physical realm right here in Polihale. They call it the house of Po. Po is the source of creation. Hale means house, right there where the vast ocean starts. The Tibetans have the same belief. The Dalai Lama insisted on visiting Polihale when he came to Hawaii, even though it wasn't even the plan for him to come to Kauai. 'This is where all souls on earth leave the physical realm,' he said."

Katie is silent for a while. "I thought you said it is always sunny here?" She points at a dark cloud, and the wind picks up.

"Oh no—the tent!" Rolf jumps up and rushes toward the green tent that floats up and bobs up and down farther and farther away from us.

The horizon is a strange palette of orange, blue, violet, and gray. As we gather the ripped pieces of the tent, an auspicious feeling arises in me. It is a mix of nervousness, calmness, and darkness. The wind seems like it is telling us something; I know that telepathic communication is multiplied in a storm.

We decide to sleep in the car. Katie and I stay in the back, and Rolf is on the front seat. The storm passes, and I feel at ease. They are both asleep, and I stare out the back window. And right then it happens. Somehow there in the back of the car, right behind my feet, right in between Katie and me I see a figure hanging in the back of the car. It is wearing a long, white nightgown. When I look again, I see it is my father. My father! My father in his familiar nightgown! *Why? Why, here?*

The answer rises out of my deepest gut. His familiar voice says, "I am going to leave my body, Christel. I want you to come home." His voice is unusually calm and strong. I hear it with no emotion at first. It just enters my whole being; it flows through me with no particular attachments. For a second, I am still in it. The nightgown is shifting. I see a strange whitish shape—little threads with white balls on it. I don't know what it means, and I don't want to know.

Right here, right now, in this place that is so associated with death, right here he appears. My father. My father who has never been sick a single day in his life! The embodiment of vitality and still so full of energy, with his always-beautiful rich, bronze tan, traveling the whole world. The sun lover. The sailor. The comedian. The always creative candy maker. Building his own boat in our garden, between the flowers, so far away from the sea, but always knowing the boat would reach it one day. And it did. In my mind, I now see the white thread with little balls on it again. I see them a little clearer now. "He has cancer," the whisper now tells me. *What? Cancer? No.*

The wind has come up, and the car is shaking again. Branches brush against the white lacquer of my Toyota. Rain pelts the windows. Adrenaline races through my veins. Here at the end of the world, a profound loneliness wells up from deep inside. I feel so far away from everything: that safe ground, the ground below sea level, the polders, the watery skies, the green pastures, and the waters of Holland. The red, white and blue striped flag above it, my parental ground. I've never felt so far away. I have to go back to Holland right away. My father wants me to come home.

***

My mother looks shorter than usual as she waits at the train station after my long flight. Is it just that I haven't seen her for a while? A slight veil of numbness covers the blue in her eyes as she drives us to the hospital.

"Here he is," she exclaims as we enter the sterile hospital room.

I look at the man in the bed and recoil. *That is not my father!* I don't recognize him. His face is swollen.

"Hallo, Ruud," my mother says, giving him a kiss.

I hobble forward, reaching for his stretched out hand.

"You act so strange," he says.

179

I want to sink in the ground from the shame of not recognizing him. I want to run hard out of this room, to the other room, where my real father is.

"I am so sorry, Papa. I hadn't expected this, you look so ... different," I whisper. "Mama only mentioned a little swelling and a bruise. Your whole face is deformed!"

My eyes trail his skinny body hooked up to the machines, his neck almost invisible.

Mad at myself, I swallow to try to hide my inadequateness.

***

A few days later, the hospital tells us that there is nothing more they can do. My father comes home. His hospital bed is in the middle of our living room.

"That boyfriend of yours—, what was his name again? He came back from death over and over again, right? He was sick and then totally healthy, right?" my father's voice sounds weak, but I see him wanting to understand.

"Yes, Umberto ... he died and came back."

"But why?"

"I will tell you the whole story, but—"

My father turns around, grabs a little box, and starts to vomit. Tears are pressing in my eyes. I have never seen my father suffering or helpless. He wipes the phlegm from his mouth and falls back on his pillow. I would rather do anything—go to the deep rain forests in the Amazon, fast for a week, put acupuncture needles in him every ten minutes—than watch him in pain. I want to tell him everything I have experienced with Umberto, the incredible version of life, this incredible journey into more of who he is, and the stripping of everything he thought was important. I feel so inadequate.

"Oh, Christel. I am so tired. Thank you for being here so quickly."

We're not allowed to open the curtains; every sound is too much. All communications are short and grumpy. It has been a week. The ideas my mother and I had to comfort him all appeared to be an illusion on the first day: the garden, the hyacinths and daffodils, the birdhouse in front of the window, and the beautiful Mozart pieces. His vocabulary becomes short commands: *poop, shoes, water.* There are no deep conversations, sweet words, deep secrets, love confessions, or words of truth.

"You guys think I am sleeping, but I am waiting to die. It takes so damn long," it is the last full sentence he says. "I am only waiting here" he repeats. "Dying takes so long. Please just let me sleep." The doctor comes the next day with morphine to let him sleep.

***

I wake up with a scream, panting. I look around, surprised that I am in my old bedroom. I see the cork walls and the reed floor. A weak moonlight enters the room. I switch the light on. I am still half in the dream. I was a boy! I was my father! A little boy assaulted. Surrounded by priests; they were grabbing my penis. I tried to push them away and yell, but a hand was put over my mouth. The squeezing—the trying to put it inside, the angry eyes—it is still all there. I feel the pain in my lower body. A catheter was inserted in my father this afternoon. It was so difficult to put in. The doctor said he never had such a problem with it. I was watching. It was painful to see. He had to try over and over, and the nurse came to try it again. My father's face was covered with pain. Tears were pouring out of his eyes—even though he was stuffed with morphine and not supposed to feel anything. He kept his eyes closed, moaning, and was barely able to lift his hand to point at his lower abdomen.

I now touch with my hand my own belly and hold it for a moment.

"It is okay. It is okay," I whisper. The next second, the pain is gone. I know it is not my pain. *I am feeling everything he is going through*—just I would with Umberto. And now it is the abuse! The abuse would surface at birthday parties with my aunts and uncles after enough wine, late at night while I was hiding under the table, as a young girl while listening to their stories. There were stories about abuse from priests, shame, rape, and scandals at boarding school. My father always kept his mouth shut. I thought it had never happened to him. I didn't want it to be true; the deeply buried pain somehow surfaced with the catheter.

I open my eyes, taking a deep breath. I traveled with him. I get a glimpse of all the layers he is going through at such a high pace. The pain, the shield, and the letting go, I feel in bliss, finally after all these awkward moments, there is that connection again. The connection with the one I always knew as my sweet papa. It doesn't matter anymore that we had no deep conversations before he got the morphine, no sweet words, no really saying good-bye, no listening to beautiful music, or watching the garden outside. He only wanted to sleep. It is his way to go through it all. And I can feel it with him—, just as with Umberto I can travel with him, I feel it all *and* the unfolding underneath it.

* * *

A few days later, my mother asks me to sleep next to my father in the living room during the night. I fall asleep quickly. In the middle of the night, I wake up with a shock. I feel a pressure on my chest. Where does it come from? A heart attack! My heart will stop any moment. In the faint light, I can see my father in the same position. His breathing is still the same. I start to breathe faster and faster. *I want to leave.* In the bathroom, I try to regain my breath. I cannot. I don't know *how* to breathe anymore! I am gasping for air. I am so afraid. I am scared! I am so scared. I am going to die! I am going to die. Help—no, that is not possible! My mother will find two dead people when she comes down in the morning! In the background, I know how absurd it is. I know I am feeling and perceiving everything that my father is feeling. I am not able to separate it. *I am my father. I am dying. I am afraid.* It races through my body.

I lay down on the stretcher again. I try to control my breathing. It has never been so spastic. I cannot find myself in my breath anymore. It is not even mine. An immense fear courses through me.

"This is not me. This is not me," I whisper, panting. I turn on the light. My father is immovable and skinny under the thin sheet, dry, rasping breath after rasping breath. There are white grains of salt on his face. I sit down next to him and take his pulse. Hard beats pound against my fingers. I try to concentrate on what I feel. *This is the death pulse.* Forceful beats push the last life force around like an uncontrolled beast. I close my eyes, and attune to my father. The pain in my own chest fades. I feel peaceful now.

"Hello, Papa. *How* are you?" I inwardly ask.

"I think this is it…" My mother now bends over him.

His breath irregular—faster and stronger. And then … my father takes his last breath. It is February 6—exactly one month after he called me from Hawaii.

Seeing Again

THERE HE IS. I reach into my shoulder bag, touch my notebook, and feel my silver pen attached to it. I take a deep breath and step toward him. My whole list of questions is ready to be asked. He is waiting under the big banyan tree. He is standing between all the big, tangled roots. I smile; it is a funny sight. He looks so small, and the root system is so big. We visited this tree in Ala Moana Park so often.

I wanted to see Umberto one more time to ask him permission to tell the story—our story—to the world. I wanted to see how things had turned out for him and how he had changed after five years of no contact, no e-mails, no messages, no phone calls, and no more dying. Since my move to Kauai, we seemed to be lifetimes away. The last time we spoke on the phone was five years ago—a week after his gallbladder attack and the operation. The last time we communicated on the computer was right before my move to Kauai. After that, it felt done. The ho'oponopono ceremony seemed to have done its job. Umberto felt released from his family karma and moved back to his birthground Jayapura. I continued my new life on Kauai.

He is on a short visit in Honolulu, and I return one more time to finish our story and write the end of my manuscript about our extraordinary experience. I fly back and forth from Kauai where my daughter is waiting for me. My three-year-old daughter is the symbol of my new life. I met Sky's father the first day I arrived in Kauai. We separated two years later, but that is another story. In five hours, my plane will leave again.

"Hi," Umberto says bashfully.

My silk dress seems too exposing for a meeting with him. I feel too naked, I realize, and I sit myself up again on my towel after I wanted to lay

183

down next to him like our bodies used to do. I lean my right hand on the grass, my legs now folded next to me, and look at him as I tug in my dress. He is bigger now; his face is more solid than I remember. It was always big, but like something was missing. He wears glasses now, which makes his eyes look different. His pupils seem not to float in eye-white anymore, but are more clearly defined. I can feel a new layer around him. It is like a protection maybe, or is it his skin that looks lighter than I remember? I wonder if I see his life in Jayapura he is living now. He wears a big watch on his left wrist, something that seems so artificial on his always- primal body. There is a strange distance between us, unknown and uncomfortable—but too subtle to name. Maybe it is the magnetic attraction underneath that we are both afraid to feel, yet it is still present.

The air is humid and stagnant, filled with vog all the way from the Big Island, which only happens on rare days with south winds. A purple haze is covering the ocean; there is no horizon visible. Even the joggers seem to go slower through the park.

He turns his face to me, moving his chin quickly up and down. "Tell me the things you wrote about me," he says. He folds his right hand over the other, squeezes it, and swallows as if he is afraid of what I am about to say. He looks afraid that it will rock the boat again for him. I almost want to comfort him and reassure him that the weight he has now, the solidness will be able to carry it all, and that we can both leave it all behind. I hesitate to pull out my notebook, deciding to make it more informal between us and leave it in my bag.

A stream of people in colorful outfits passes by in the distance. They are walking, running, on bikes, and on skates. The smell of the fresh-mowed grass circles us. He is almost like a stranger to me, but it is good.

"I am almost done with it," I say. "It took me three years to write it all down. Now I just need the ending. I came to Honolulu today to see you—just to see the real you one more time. I wonder how you are doing now. When I was writing it all down, I didn't want to know. I was afraid it would disturb it—or that you would die again. You went into a coma seven times, and you died four times. The first time with the tsunami, then both your lung operations, the alcohol overdose, then the gallbladder and—"

"The doctor says I am totally healthy now," he whispers. "Not a trace."

"That is so unbelievable. I always said you were a delog, but you denied it. That is what delogs do. They die—or go into a deep coma—and they come back without any trace of damage. The clearing on the other side creates immediate healing in the body. I was the witness behind my laptop of the clearing and the places you went."

"Wow. I just remember hearing you and smelling your scent." He shakes his head.

A tear starts to appear in the corner of his eye, as he now holds his head so still. As if moving it would destroy the memory, just like when waking up with a dream. He stares in the distance next to me. Another tear appears. I can see the memories come back to him, like he almost had forgotten about them. He takes off his glasses, and I look at the droplet of salty water still lingering in the corner of his eye, as if hoping to see the kaleidoscope of images of his memory reflected in the drop. Then he wipes his tears away forcefully.

I take a short pause, a big yellow leaf falls from the banyan tree above us. I continue to tell him the story about what happened with my father, six months ago in January.

"I had learned so much through the experience with you, but now I felt so incapable with my own father—, my own flesh and blood," I told Umberto. "It felt impossible to convey that what I had learned. Seeing the reality of my father's body in front of me and feeling the terrible pain of losing him, made me realize how it could have never happened between you and me the way it did if we were on the same island, in close proximity. My father just kept on asking me the question, 'Why was Umberto able to come back over and over again? Why I am not able to heal like him?' And I could not give him an answer. It was so painful. I felt such a failure not being able to provide a solid answer, at the same time seeing my own father—, the love of my life— slide away. Yes, why? Why? I wondered."

"Did he accept it in the end?" Umberto looks at me intently now.

"I told him about the orange butterfly, and that made him accept it. I would see a big black moth when you were in a coma, and I would see an orange butterfly around me after my father appeared to me in Polihale. It just seemed to follow me everywhere. I asked why, and to my surprise, it told me very clearly that it was Angele, his oldest sister. She told me she came to guide my father to the other side. She said she had a promise to keep. My aunt had felt so far away after she passed away five years earlier. When I told all this to my father, he burst into tears for the first time. He said how much it meant to him. I didn't know that Angele made a promise to him on her deathbed that she would reward him for all the work he had done in her last days. It was such a validation for him that she kept her promise—and that was when he could surrender."

Umberto nods slowly, pushing his lips together as if trying to hold something inside. I can see the struggle he has when I name my aunt Angele. The one he prayed for with the whole church and who didn't want a bible in her head.

"From that moment on, it was just like with you. I was able to experience it with him—not on the computer or through letters on my screen—in my body and my senses when he was going through so many layers. I learned so much about him in that short time: his pain, old memories from childhood, abuse by priests at his school, fears, longings, and emotions. There were things I didn't even know of. It was such a liberation to see that there were no limitations. It was a liberation of the one he always thought he was into a bigger version of him. I could feel it all rising. His heart opened. I could feel my heart opening with his. That stayed for weeks and months after his passing. *Now I am really able to fall in love*, I thought for the first time."

"Really?" Umberto smiles for the first time. He takes off his glasses, and with that the mask leaves. He has permission to peel it off. All that was familiar between us floats back in. Our energetic tendrils suddenly unfurl and embrace each other again. The closeness, the attraction, the ground we shared, the shared experience of how magic life actually is, despite all our differences, it all comes back. The same magic that had pulled me to Hawaii in the first place, the blind kahuna woman on the Big Island talked about. I touch his arm with three fingers.

He gets up and reaches his hand out to me. "Get up. Let's get moving. We could get a tea at the Chinese restaurant and then go to my friend's house where I stay. We have three more hours."

"Okay," I hoist myself up.

When we start walking back to the path, he reaches out his hand.

I touch it gently; the palm of my hand softly feels into the pinkness of the inside of his. I rub it, with my fingers stretched. The strange familiarity as if we are brother and sister returns. Gently I fold my fingers around his. Sensing his gait again next to me, like we did so many times. Like it felt when he was on the other side.

"You know what?" he says. "A few years ago, I was here in Honolulu for a short visit from Jayapura. I saw you with your dog—right here in the park. You were walking toward me, straight over the field. And then you turned and walked away from me. It made my heart break. I felt like I'd lost you forever—even though we were not together. I felt so heavy. I wasn't even able to run after you, but your dog kept on looking at me. Was that really you? I thought it was just a wish."

I stop, let go of his hand, and look at him in disbelief. "Really? Yes, it was me and Layka! I was here with her on Oahu for two weeks. I was trying to get her pregnant with Kooiker semen from Texas. She was in heat, and I found a vet who would inseminate her on the North Shore. I wanted to show Layka all the places I went with you—all the beaches and all the parks. I thought you were in Papua. I couldn't believe it when I saw you approaching me. I couldn't believe Layka was looking at you so intensely. I thought it was a dream. I couldn't explain why Layka kept on looking back at you that way. When I looked back, you seemed to have vanished. I tried to call you when I got back to my car, but your phone was disconnected. And the e-mail I sent later that day bounced."

We look at each other for a few moments with our mouths open and eyes wide. We hold still and try to let in the reality of the experience. The only witness, Layka, was undeniably seeing the same thing. Umberto saw her looking at him, and I saw her looking at Umberto even when I turned away. I had denied the whole experience right after.

"Did she get pregnant?" Umberto breaks the strange silence as he continues walking.

"No." I laugh. "But that is another story ... a big story."

***

"Every family has a mythology," Umberto says, lying on his side with his arms folded across his chest. The pillow pushes his glasses away from his face in a funny angle. We are back in Waikiki, back in the "unknown water." We are at his friend Randy's house. We have two hours before I fly back to Kauai. The room is clear and neat, painted in a soft yellow, with big mirrors with golden rims on the wall and a thick white carpet, just like in Lennard's house. It is so different than all the dark caves he was living in with friends before.

"What do you mean?"

"Now that I am living in Papua, I get to know so much about the history of my father. I realize how everybody has a role and a story about how they came to be who they are. So much comes from family. I learned so much about the background of my Papuan family."

"What mythology?" I hear a slight tremble in my voice. I think of all the therapies, family constellations, and groups I have done to get rid of my family story. I rise above that old limited view of myself, not to carry their drama anymore. Ancestral programming has played such a powerful role in the past, but I believe it is time to rise above it and awaken to a truer nature of who we are.

Umberto's family drama is so present in everything he does.

Living in Hawaii seems to have made Umberto's Hawaiian background play out, the whole curse with the Big Island. Since he moved back to his paternal ground, it looks like a whole new part in him is activated. I see it in the different shine on his skin. I hold my breath for a moment, wondering what he is about to say. That mysterious part of him always gave me a little bit the creeps: his Papuan background.

"You know my last name, right? Sihirbaz. I had this strong curiosity about my ancestors, my grandfather and his forefathers and the name they were carrying. That is why I moved back to Papua. And you know what it means? Sihirbaz means trickster—the one who plays games with the gods. I told you about the abilities my grandfather had, right? That he was able to actually manifest stones falling out of the air in times of invasions in our town? Well, since I returned to Papua, I started to have dreams and visions about my family. It was really weird. I wanted to spend as much time in nature as possible, and it all came back suddenly. A month ago, I was in a forest I always went to with my grandfather. I was sitting down, and all of a sudden, these vines started to grow around me. They were like snakes. They were holding me down, I couldn't move. That was when I started to get this vision." He holds his breath again, reaches out to the string from my dress around my neck, and pulls it toward him. He sighs and lets it go like a rubber band.

"My family was a kind of mischievous; they were able to create illusions that appeared to be so real. They could manifest spirits in everything they wanted. They were so admired, but people didn't know what to believe anymore. They became angry at my family because it was like they were challenging the gods."

"Man, that sounds just like your mother's history."

"Worse." His voice is deep and abrupt.

"Worse?" A strange chill travels my limbs. I see that line again from my astrocartography chart—straight through Papua—and I hear the words of my astrologer friend Grace. "This symbolizes the wound in your chart ... the most painful part and the gift within."

"They became outcasts and outlaws."

"Is that why you want to live as ordinarily as possible—because you can feel it coming after you too?" In the back of my mind, I realize what a great idea it was to come to Oahu to get these last pieces of information. I will now be able to write the end of my book, and that will be it. In a few hours, I will be reunited with my daughter and my Dutch friend, Esther who is watching her. We will laugh about it all: Umberto's mythology.

"So, if your mythology is the trickster, what would be my mythology?"

We stare at each other now looking into each other's eyes, and I sense we are both trying to gauge how truthful this question should be, as if it would unveil a new, naked truth if we really let it. I almost regret the question.

He rolls on his back and looks at the ceiling. His hands are crossed over his chest.

For a moment, I cannot but imagine his hands lay like that on his dead body so many times before.

"Unobtainable."

The way he says it hits me: dry and neutral, almost robotic, but with so much charge. He sums it all up in that one word and sheds a whole new light on everything.

I swallow.

I see him close his eyes behind his glasses.

"Umberto, but ..." I try to speak. *Unobtainable?* Did he mean he was always trying to win me, and that is why he died? Is he still trying to obtain me? His words are like a dark hook in my unbroken white flesh—straight through my green silk dress. In my mind, my body is back on Kauai already, united with my daughter and laughing with my friend. *Unobtainable?* I thought he would be over that.

But how unobtainable am I really? He is right, in a way. I have been unobtainable for my whole life. With Lennard—, and all my lovers—, I always felt above them somehow, and it was a good thing—, just like with my daughter's father. I never let them in too far, get too vulnerable, too attached, or even more let them affect my path. I never wanted a man to be in the way of establishing myself in Hawaii. I had told myself over and over again that I would really open myself to a man when I felt rooted in Hawaii. Guilt now starts to creep out of me, which I didn't know I had. I feel guilty about my thoughts. I feel guilty, about already wanting to go back to Kauai with the last notes for my book. I feel guilty, guilty about not really wanting to connect to him today. I feel guilty, guilty about always being on another island. I feel guilty even more, that I am on a far away island and not with my good friends back in Holland. Not being with my husband Lennard.

I think about climbing on top of him and kissing him.

I could tell him how it all has changed now when my father died, how I feel I can really open my heart now. But what he wants is impossible. He still wants us to love each other equally.

I slide myself across the sheets, hook one leg over him, sit up so I am straddling him like I would a horse and look down at him. He took off his glasses, and holds them in his outstretched hand. In his eyes, I can see a helplessness I so remember from him: the floating, as if unable to grab onto something, anything. In his eyes I can see even more of his strong ancestral energy. It holds the middle ground between tremendous powers and abilities and an incredible emotional pain. He drops his glasses, and his hands come up now to clasp my thighs. Sitting on him almost becomes awkward. I feel so above him again, but I am afraid moving away will make him feel like another rejection. So I hold still. He gently slides his fingers up my legs and lifts up my dress.

I feel myself melt into something so familiar. *Please let me lose myself in you for one last time. Let me jump beyond the safety I found for a moment.*

Let me show you that I am not unobtainable. Just drag me there for the short hours I am here with you. Take me out of my remote heart, the cold stone castle, the tower of the witness, the arrogance of being above it.

The sweat—the liquid of our hearts—oozes out of us. Our insides become outside, and a glowing film appears around our bodies. The light on my curves shines. The sweat is lubricating our naked bodies as the juice of our desire.

I can see the steam, the colorful haze around us, showing more than we knew we were just a few minutes ago. I feel the longing for the unknown, the magic, and the darkness of the unknown water.

I can see your erectness like a hungry wolf. My red mouth spreads open. I can feel you inside of me now.

And then, … there they are. There they are again, faces appear all around you—and all around the bed. Different faces now, even more to the surface. I recognize them now as different—the culture of the land you moved back to. Papua is your father's ground. And with our lovemaking, it seems like we are inviting it all in now.

The Trickster

IT IS NOVEMBER 2012, Sky and I kneel in our new little garden—next to the guava tree. She is four. We are next to the little purple flowers we just planted; our bare feet are in the dirt. Our little red bungalow is right next to us. There is no moon tonight. It is almost dark. Layka sniffs the grass behind us. The waves of the ocean sound strong tonight. I sigh. I am happy we found our place so close by. We did not have to leave the bay. We did not have to leave Moloa'a. I got to love this place so much. The day I was evicted, this bungalow across the street magically opened up at only a fraction of the rent I had to pay before.

"Where do the colors go at night, Mama?" In the weak light, she points at the flowers.

"We cannot see the colors with our eyes, Sky. It is swallowed up by the darkness. Darkness absorbs color, but it is just an illusion." *Just like Umberto swallowed it all up.*

On the other side of the street, our old green house is visible. The lights go on. I swallow; the day after I met Umberto in Honolulu, he sent me a text message: "I am in a coma. Please help me. I need money for medicine."

I was surprised that it sounded so desperate. The letters didn't come outside any frame, were not in cursive, were not about heavenly creatures, and were not an exact description of the feelings I was going through. It started with asking for money for medicine to get him out of his coma, and then he started to ask for money for operations. He moved the stakes even higher when he told me he was not going to be back in his body. He wanted to put his will in my name and leave me all the money he inherited from his family. He asked for money to pay a lawyer. And I did. I believed it all.

I sent Umberto $14,000 dollars. Scraping away my last money, the money I made from giving retreats. And while I had never been late on rent or car payments ever before in my life, now I got evicted from my house, my brand new Toyota Highlander was repossessed.

There was no smell in our communications. There was no sound, no sensing him, no seeing him, no butterflies, no special effects on my screen, no flying laptop, and no expansive feeling of bliss.

I didn't allow myself to feel. There was only the discomfort in my gut, the discomfort that I didn't want to listen to. I wanted to rationalize it. The discomfort that they name at the Sixth Sense Center as "not your own energy." It's a sign that something is taking away your authority, that you *let* something take away your authority. The whisper told me one thing, at the bank: "Here you are like a junkie—addicted, sending him more money, and keeping the circle of fear alive."

I was not able to feel anymore, I was narrowed down to the same place that Umberto kept on describing to me at the same time: a small cage, being held captive by scary creatures, that looked like half lizard half human, creating extreme fear. I was not immune to it this time: the fear that made me so small. Like an illness, it came into me, like a virus, it attached, like snakes, it was eating away all my discernment: I believed it all—, despite the warnings of my friends.

I was mesmerized again, and there was no Shen to help me. He had said, "I am going to help you only once." And now my Dantian was stolen again. The irony was that my Qigong teacher had left his body at the same time Umberto started betraying me. Shen died so consciously. He had asked his students to meditate for him and say a mantra each day of the forty-nine days so he would not get stuck in the near-earth realms, not get stuck in the games we play on earth, the lower vibrations of ignorance and greed, manipulations and abuse of power. Instead, he would move into the higher realms—beyond ancestral programming—in a grander freedom, beyond his identity, beyond everything he believed he was.

Jhampa the Tibetan doctor had told me twenty years ago that at the end of the forty-nine days of the soul traveling through the "in-between state," the ancestors have their final opportunity to yank the soul back into their story, into their family mythology. I felt I had landed now with Umberto at the end of our journey, and here it was: his Papuan ancestry. They pulled him right back in; back into the mythology of the trickster and the craft of illusion. Now he tricked me into it, making it appear so real— no matter how conscious or unconscious it was for him.

Finally, I realized: it was all a lie this time. I felt my whole life sink when I saw a picture of Umberto on Facebook. He was not dead. He was alive. When I reached him on the phone, he admitted it all with a monotonous voice; after he had seen me in Honolulu, he wanted to obtain me. "I don't know why I did it," he said, "I just couldn't stop it any more." He gave me the tiniest sorry and the promise to pay it all back.

After that, I broke all contact with him.

Then the questions arose. *Was it then all not true? Was it then all an illusion?* Over and over again I went through it in my mind: all the undeniable things we went through, and the line of brilliance unfolding before my very eyes. Almost perfectly orchestrated, the message out of my pen that in a way had told me so clearly, I was the witness seeing heaven going digital. And yes, it did expand my consciousness tremendously. I asked myself over and over again: Did that really happen? Yes, that did really happen, I had to conclude over and over again.

And I was able to sense the same communication, the same closeness, and the same urging to choose with my oma, and her stepping out of her mist. And after that, it was the deeply sensuous experience with my own father slipping away – I could experience it all with him just like I had done with Umberto and learn this time so much about who my father really was and where he was going. The tremendous richness of the experience remained.

But how could Umberto have changed so much that he went to heaven and hell, saw it all, experienced it all, was the modern delog, with prophecies, holy guides, clearly appearing on my computer screen, and still scammed me? It kept me in the illusion, numbing my intuition and my sensitivities. The sexual force had lured me into it this time—the strong bond we had recreated in Honolulu and the access I gave him to have power over me. He became the shark on the other side the dark predator side, instead of the light side. I had seen him doing it over and over again. He changed from the soft, friendly boy to a hard, metallic, cold, and aggressive predator. The predator finally obtained me between his teeth.

I look up at our old house again. The lights go out.

My daughter looks up at me. "But is the flower still blooming, Mama?"

"Yes, it is still blooming. And some flowers only bloom at night. Come, I will let you smell the night-blooming jasmine here in our new yard." I stand up and grab my daughter's little hand.

Author's Bio

CHRISTEL JANSSEN (1969, the Netherlands) is a Qigong teacher and licensed acupuncturist. She blends her extended knowledge of Chinese and Tibetan Medicine with her intuitive abilities and experience. She is the founder of the Virtual School for Spontaneous Movement with online intuitive classes and she offers Spontaneous Movement Writers Retreats in Hawaii 'to allow a bigger reality to speak through you' . Visit her website:

christeljanssen.com

spontaneousmovement.com

This book is also available as an Audiobook on Audible and iTunes. Narrated by the author.

72644493R00133

Made in the USA
Lexington, KY
01 December 2017